Witch

Praise for *Witch*

'Lisa Lister is an uber-goddess of humour, wisdom, fun and cheek. She's just what THIS doctor ordered.'
DR CHRISTIANE NORTHRUP, AUTHOR OF *GODDESSES NEVER AGE* AND *MAKING LIFE EASY*

'Reclaim that which is lost. Fall inwards and away from that which we have been sold and doesn't serve us. We are women, deep and wise, and Lisa Lister is a woman walking us into this wisdom. I love Lisa. I love everything she writes. I love her voice, her way, her magic. She weaves the truth and busts through the myths so that we can reclaim our true power. *Witch* is for every women who aches and knows that there is another way.'
CARRIE ANNE MOSS, ACTRESS AND FOUNDER OF ANNAPURNALIVING.COM

'*Witch* is what we all remember when we close our eyes, when we're unafraid to own our power, when no one and nothing outside of us is as convincing as the force of light we can only find within. *Witch* is a reclamation, a reparation and mostly a revelation that love cannot be burned or buried. The love that witches have always been can only ever rise, and expand. *Witch* reveals a lineage of love we inherit when we dare to fully embody and become unapologetic about how much we know.'
MEGGAN WATTERSON, AUTHOR OF *REVEAL* AND *HOW TO LOVE YOURSELF*

'Being a witch isn't just a decision – it's a calling, and I am certain that Lisa Lister has spent many lifetimes preparing for this call. Lisa is a real witch who dares to shed light on a spiritual craft that shows reverence for women, nature and spirit. Let Lisa and this book be the medicine you need to awaken the witch in you.'
KYLE GRAY, BESTSELLING AUTHOR OF *WINGS OF FORGIVENESS* AND *RAISE YOUR VIBRATION*

'Lisa Lister is a badass leader of all things feminine. She is here to shine a light on all the shadows of patriarchy that we have all inherited. *Witch* is a book whose time has come and a response to the feminine that is rising within us all. Rise sister rise.'
REBECCA CAMPBELL, BESTSELLING AUTHOR OF *LIGHT IS THE NEW BLACK* AND *RISE SISTER RISE*

'Check your unicorn into a stable and find some chocolate for your fairy because you won't be needing them here. Lisa's writing in this new offering, *Witch*, is powerful, raw and challenging, just as it should be. This book is more than words on a page, it's Lisa's blood, sweat and tears infusing every glorious moment that will take you deeper into yourself, deep enough to meet the only magical being you truly ever need to know – yourself.'

DAVID WELLS, ASTROLOGER AND AUTHOR OF *QABALAH* AND *PAST PRESENT AND FUTURE*

'Lisa Lister is the woman we all wish we were lucky enough to have as our sister. But short of having her on speed dial, this book is the next best thing to a full-on feminine support system!'

KATHLEEN MCGOWAN, ACTIVIST AND INTERNATIONAL BESTSELLING AUTHOR OF *THE EXPECTED ONE* AND *THE BOOK OF LOVE*

'Lisa is one of those rare human beings who not only teaches truth and vitality and vulnerability and divinity, but actually **embodies** it. I love her work. I love her. *Witch* will change you, empower you, guide you on your journey to deeper acknowledgment of who you are and why you came here. Let it work its magic on you.'

HOLLIE HOLDEN, FOUNDER OF *NOTES ON LIVING AND LOVING*

'When someone as bold, brazen and erudite as Lisa Lister emerges to propose women feel pride in all their aspects and functions, we must afford her all the support we can muster. For if we are to evolve as a species now, it will be the women who lead us in it, ideally with the support and help of the men, but certainly no longer in deference to them.'

BAREFOOT DOCTOR, AUTHOR OF *BAREFOOT DOCTOR'S HANDBOOK FOR THE URBAN WARRIOR*

'Lisa Lister is love on fire. A true embodiment of the Goddess on Earth who walks the fire path of love, truth and fleshly feelings of wild desire – women wake to an unconditional and healing love in Lisa's wake. Her words, all from the deepest caverns of her heart, touch the hearts of all who read her. To read Lisa is to know her, and to know Lisa is to know oneself. Her journey is yours, and yours hers, and all together we piece the Goddess back together on the planet.'

SARAH DURHAM WILSON, FOUNDER OF DOITGIRL.COM AND AUTHOR OF *THE DO IT GIRL DIARIES*

Witch

UNLEASHED.
UNTAMED.
UNAPOLOGETIC.

LISA LISTER

HAY HOUSE

Carlsbad, California • New York City • London
Sydney • Johannesburg • Vancouver • New Delhi

First published and distributed in the United Kingdom by:
Hay House UK Ltd, Astley House, 33 Notting Hill Gate, London W11 3JQ
Tel: +44 (0)20 3675 2450; Fax: +44 (0)20 3675 2451; www.hayhouse.co.uk

Published and distributed in the United States of America by:
Hay House Inc., PO Box 5100, Carlsbad, CA 92018-5100
Tel: (1) 760 431 7695 or (800) 654 5126; Fax: (1) 760 431 6948 or (800) 650 5115
www.hayhouse.com

Published and distributed in Australia by:
Hay House Australia Ltd, 18/36 Ralph St, Alexandria NSW 2015
Tel: (61) 2 9669 4299; Fax: (61) 2 9669 4144
www.hayhouse.com.au

Published and distributed in the Republic of South Africa by:
Hay House SA (Pty) Ltd, PO Box 990, Witkoppen 2068
info@hayhouse.co.za; www.hayhouse.co.za

Published and distributed in India by:
Hay House Publishers India, Muskaan Complex, Plot No.3, B-2,
Vasant Kunj, New Delhi 110 070
Tel: (91) 11 4176 1620; Fax: (91) 11 4176 1630; www.hayhouse.co.in

Distributed in Canada by:
Raincoast Books, 2440 Viking Way, Richmond, B.C. V6V 1N2
Tel: (1) 604 448 7100; Fax: (1) 604 270 7161; www.raincoast.com

Text © Lisa Lister, 2017

The moral rights of the author have been asserted.

The information given in this book should not be treated as a substitute for professional medical advice; always consult a medical practitioner. Any use of information in this book is at the reader's discretion and risk. Neither the author nor the publisher can be held responsible for any loss, claim or damage arising out of the use, or misuse, of the suggestions made, the failure to take medical advice or for any material on third party websites.

A catalogue record for this book is available from the British Library.

ISBN: 978-1-78180-754-5

Certified Chain of Custody
SUSTAINABLE FORESTRY INITIATIVE
Promoting Sustainable Forestry
www.sfiprogram.org
SFI-01268

SFI label applies to the text stock

Contents

Now is the time

This is the hour,

Ours is the magic

Ours is the power.

– The Craft, 1996

Introduction

Women, we are living in 'interesting times'.

Society, nature and the way we interact with each other are *all* changing. There's a quickening, and many of us – more than ever before – are hearing 'The Call'.

I spoke about The Call in my last book, *Love Your Lady Landscape*. It's…

The Call from SHE, the divine feminine.

The Call to rise, fully rooted, in the truth of who we are.

The Call that asks us to trust ourselves.

It's The Call to trust our gut, our intuition, our pussy-power and our innate feminine wisdom. It's The Call to know that when we do, our current, out-of-date hierarchical structures will crumble. Slowly at first, but they *will* crumble.

Yeah, THAT call.

For many, hearing The Call will feel like a remembrance – maybe of a past life, maybe of a whisper from an ancestor, maybe of a feeling deep in your bones. Either way, it's a remembrance of who you were before you forgot.

It's a remembrance of who you were before Patriarchy put all your fierce and feminine powers into the darkness, called them taboo and then taught you to be afraid of the dark.

This remembrance is waking the witches.

Witch, a term that has previously been used to demonize, stigmatize and repress women, is now being reclaimed. Women across the globe are now actively using it as a way to describe themselves.

Yep, in a world where the word 'witch' has previously conjured up images of wart-faced old women huddled around a cauldron, the witch has undergone a serious image overhaul in the 21st century. Far from being about practising the dark arts, the modern witch movement is all about female empowerment.

Women are gathering in circles – both online and offline – to celebrate the different phases of the moon cycle. They're performing rituals to honour the seasons, and casting spells to heal, to manifest and to rediscover their magic.

The witch is waking.

The witch represents the part of each of us that has been censored, ignored, punished and demonized. And it's a part that wants – no, *needs* – to be accessed and fully expressed.

I regularly get asked, 'Why do you think women are fearful to speak out, to be heard and to fully express themselves?'

My answer? It's because we're fearful of the witch inside each and every one of us.

The witch is a woman *fully* in her power.

She's in touch with the dark. She knows how to be the witness, how to let things go and how to follow her own counsel. Most importantly though, she questions EVERYTHING.

She's connected, pussy to the Earth.

She hears the whispers of those who have gone before her, and she feels the ancient secrets that are in her bones. She's the one who knows *without fail* that there's more to this life than actually meets the eye.

She causes hierarchical power structures to shake in her wake.

She knows that in any given moment, she can be a hot mess, a woman of grace and beauty, angry and grief-struck, loved and pleasure-sated, tired and soft or raw and vulnerable.

She also knows that in some moments, she can be all of these at once.

She's whole.

And a woman who's whole? Well, she's a really bloody *scary* threat to anyone who's not in full integrity – not fully aligned with the truth of who they are and what they stand for. Ourselves and our own delicate egos included, right?

The witch is re-membering (reintegrating all the parts of herself that have been dis-membered, to make herself whole again) and re-wilding.

The part of us that was once anaesthetized, domesticated and kept numb by food (or by shopping, drugs and the media) is now awakening in each of us. And it's our wholeness, our intuition, our magic and our power – the power that lies between our thighs – that will *truly* change the world.

And so witches, it's time to wake.
It's time to re-member.
For ourselves and for our planet.

It's time to re-member that to be a witch is to be a powerful woman in a world where women have, for thousands of years until now, felt really bloody powerless.

Which is why, when the 'modern' witch – the one who wears dark lipstick and a silver crescent moon crown and has a bra-full of crystals – gets a broomstick beating from a more 'traditional witch', I have to call it out.

Sure, it might be tempting to write someone off as 'superficial' or to accuse them of turning being a 'witch' into just another empty, consumable fad; but beneath all that glossy packaging is a woman waking to her power.

So honestly? It doesn't matter whether you call yourself a witch because a magazine did a two-page spread inspired by the movie

The Craft (I freakin' LOVE that movie!), or because you're a hereditary witch from a lineage that taught you to read tarot, use herbs and make tinctures for spells (that's what I am). Either way, know this: calling yourself a witch is a big-ass responsibility.

It carries power.

SHE power.

Reclaiming the word and identifying as a witch *will* call your power back, because being a witch runs bone-deep.

As women, we carry the stories – the pain and the fear – of the women who've gone before us.

We carry the stories of women who were persecuted, burned, drowned, tortured and silenced because of their power; and we carry it in our very DNA. So waking and reclaiming the witch within us takes really big ovaries.

If you want to do this, it takes a womb-deep recognition that you are:

- A woman who is powerful. You bleed for five days and don't die: don't tell me that doesn't make you a superhero.

- A Force of Nature who knows the ebb and flow of the moon, the seasons, Mumma Nature and her own body – and is able to use all of them for good.

- A Creatrix who can manifest and make the magic that's needed on the planet right now.

- An Oracle with seer-like vision, intuition and foresight.

- A Healer who creates the balm needed to help heal the huge, gaping wound that Patriarchy has caused.

- A Sorceress who can both charm and be dangerous.

It's this simple; If you call yourself a witch, you've got to be ready to deal with everything that comes with it. It's a lesson that Sarah Durham Wilson – my friend, witch and coven sister (this lifetime and many lifetimes before) – and I discuss and experience over and over again.

That's why I'm writing this book.

Everything I share in this book is a reclamation project by order of SHE, the Goddess, the Mother God.

It will call us ALL to take fierce responsibility in reclaiming the word 'witch' and all that it represents and symbolizes. Oh, and FYI, being a witch has *nothing* to do with how you dress, what crystal you use or what your witch lineage is.

Instead, it's about being a woman who can recognize, navigate, claim, trust and use her Goddess-given powers of creativity and manifestation, her vision, her intuition and foresight, her rhythms and cyclic nature and her ability to experience FULLY the dark to serve the light. And she does it to heal not only herself, but her family, her community and ultimately, the world.

Forget history, AKA 'His Story'. This book is a re-membering, re-writing and re-telling of HER Story.

This is the greatest story NEVER told. It's OUR story.

This book is a response to the fact that for centuries, women have been persecuted for their power. The fact that women like my nanna were forced to speak in hushed tones about the magic that they made. The fact that women like my mum turned their back on their power and gave it away completely for fear of shame and judgement.

It's our responsibility as women who live in this time and place to reclaim the word 'witch', and to respond to all that it calls up in us.

Are you ready?

Then step into the fire – the same fire that was once used to silence us. Let all the fear, pain, anger and injustice *burn*.

Feel its heat licking at your toes.

Now, claim your power and wake the witch.

It's time.

It's time to gather in circles in order to remember your truth, your wisdom and your true nature.

It's time to trust yourself and to trust each other.

It's time to connect with Nature, with Mumma Earth and her cycles, and with the liminal space between it all.

It's time to connect with SHE, the divine feminine. To remember that SHE is us, and that we are SHE.

It's time to connect with HE, the divine masculine, because wholeness is what we're all seeking.

This is how it always was; and in order to restore the balance in ourselves and on the planet, it's how it has to be again.

Come join me in circle; because woman, it's time. THIS is the witching hour.

Lisa x

About This Book

This book is pretty much *my* vision, the way that *I* do things.

It'll be different from many other witches' traditions, but you'll find it similar in a lot of ways too.

There are many ways to *be* a witch, and the word means different things to different people.

My suggestion?

Don't get too caught up in the details.

Read this book from cover to cover, use it as a divination tool or sleep with it under your pillow. Whatever you do, know that what I share in these pages is my experience and my practice.

I am not every woman. I am not every witch.

Some parts of the book will call to you loudly because you'll be remembering what you already know. Other parts you may find yourself disagreeing with wildly, and that's totally okay. I don't write books to tell you how you 'should' do things, I write them to spark a fire of recognition and remembrance in your womb, gut and body.

It's what you decide to do with what you remember that makes the real magic happen.

NOTE: I talk a lot in the book about how the witch is non-apologetic for who she is. Yet, as I was pulling my pages and pages of handwritten notes into book form, I felt an overwhelming need to apologize for writing a book specifically about women as witches.

I thought:

… I'll piss off traditional witches because I'm not being 'witchy' enough.

… I'll piss off Pagans for not being inclusive of all the possible paths.

… I'll piss off men for not addressing them as witches.

… I'll piss off the transgender community for not addressing them either.

Yet this is the work I do.

I do women's work, and I'm definitely not going to apologize for *that*.

That thought? That need to apologize? That's the very reason why I HAVE to write this book.

What I share is NOT intended to exclude others. But trying to be *all-inclusive* would totally miss the point. It would feel like I was bypassing the particular story that I believe needs to be told; because while some incredible, brave and courageous women have come before us and paved the way, there's still a lot of work to be done.

To play our part in dismantling the Patriarchy – the construct that wants to keep us separate and disconnected from ourselves and each other – we need to remember the Goddess-given tools and power we were born with.

I'm a hereditary witch, meaning I was born into a family who practised their own form of Gypsy magic. I turned my back on it for a few years to do the 'important work' – ahem – of following boy bands, kissing and being a teenager who wasn't laughed at for being the 'Gypsy kid'.

But then, when my nanna died, she spoke to me often through the dreamtime; and she kept encouraging me to come back to my magic.

So, as with most things I do, I got geeky about it.

I've studied not just the practices of my own Gypsy tradition, but witchcraft in *all* its forms for over 10 years now, including:

- The Stregheria of Italy
- The roots and bones of Hoodoo

- Shamankas

- Mayan medicine women

- Gardnerian and Alexandrian traditions of Wicca

So now my personal practice has become pretty eclectic; but ultimately, at my core, I worship the Mother God. I also, rather controversially, call in Mary Magdalene and Kali Ma as my coven sister witches.

I use the seasons of Mumma Nature, the cycles of the moon and my own menstrual cycle to connect and hone my craft.

I cast spells, work with plant medicine and love nothing more than to stand naked under a full moon and howl.

Arrrooooooooooo.

The 'craft' today is built on the sense that witchcraft and the old ways have been lost, buried and/or corrupted. That means it's up to women like you and me to attempt to rediscover them and make them relevant to the world we live in now.

To me, the essence of a witch is someone who trusts their inner authority and uses their own personal magic to navigate and negotiate the environment they currently find themselves in.

This, I'm sure, will invoke a lot of eye-rolling from traditionalists and those who practise specific traditions of the craft. So be it.

In this book, I'll introduce you to some of the many traditions of witchcraft and their practices. You'll find spells to try, and pages from my own Book of Shadows... but just to be super clear: none of it is *actually* necessary.

They're just prompts to remind you to trust yourself, to go back to the root of the craft – the craft of the wise, the craft of the wise woman – where witches were female shamans who worked with dreamtime, visions, herbs and incantations.

NOTE: I'm not suggesting that you ditch your iPhone and drop social media to revert back to the old ways. Instead, I'm asking you to remember and then make that remembrance relevant for your life today.

We're so used to being given a five-point plan or instructions on how to do everything that we no longer trust ourselves. So what I'm suggesting is that you let everything you read in this book be a cosmic wink – a cheeky broomstick prod to trust your heart, your gut and your womb space to be your guide.

You don't need an intermediary to connect with source and your inner wisdom. Simply put your feet on Mumma Earth, get still or create a prayer or incantation.

Honestly, the most powerful and effective spells you'll ever work will be the ones you create yourself. They'll be specifically tuned to your requirements, and charged with your own brand of creativity, passion and lady magic.

So I invite you to experience reading this book as though you're part of a not-so-secret coven.

I want it to feel like, no matter where you are in the world, and no matter what time of day it is, when you open the book up to read, you're sitting in a circle that's been ritually opened by a guide-ess who walks the path and all its edges.

I want it to feel like you're surrounded by a coven of like-minded wise women, healers and medicine keepers – witches – and as though behind you are all the women that have gone before you, right back to the beginning of time.

All of us are there, holding you, supporting you and loving you, as you read and ready yourself to become a fully awakened witch and reclaim your power.

Before I enter a circle, I always take a ritual bath; and that's where I recommend you start.

⚬ A RITUAL BATH ⚬

The purpose of this bath is to cleanse you of negative energies and prepare your physical, mental and spiritual self for circle. You'll usually perform this rite just before you step into circle: it's medicine for the witch, healing for the healer, and a way to soak fully in the power and presence of your own being.

This is a ritual bath that I personally use before circles; but trust yourself, witch. Let your intuition guide you to the herbs and oils that YOU need right now.

(Of course, be sure to check for contraindications if you have any specific health conditions or are currently pregnant.)

What you'll need:

- Sacred water (I'm blessed that I regularly visit Glastonbury, a town here in the UK that's steeped in magic and lore. I'll often collect water from both the Red and the White spring there each time I visit, but honestly? Sacred water is any water that's natural to Mumma Earth: seawater, spring water or river water. Or, if you're landlocked, make your own sacred water by adding salt to tap water and putting it on your altar to bless it before using it.)

- Pink Himalayan Salt or Epsom Salts

- Three sprigs of rosemary

- A rose quartz crystal

- Red and pink rose petals

- Any herbs that you feel particularly called to add (check out the Witch's Herbal in Chapter 11)

- Rose absolute oil

- A candle

- Wine or another libation of your choice to be drunk at the end of the rite

What to do:

Infuse your bath water with three small cups of Himalayan bath salt, the rose quartz, the rosemary sprigs, a few drops of your sacred water, the rose petals and five or six drops of the rose absolute oil.

Anoint the candle with the rose absolute oil, then light it.

Lower yourself into the water, and visualize it cleansing you of all negative vibes. Know that these energies are flowing from your physical, mental and spiritual self into the water. Relax and enjoy the warmth of the water, the scents in the air and the feeling of being cleansed of all negativity.

Let yourself drift.

As you bathe, take a moment to set an intention and concentrate on the purpose of your ritual. Why did you buy this book? Are you ready to wake the witch within? To claim the title 'witch' fully as your own?

Visualize your purpose, and know that you are truly prepared.

When you feel ready, pull the plug and stay in the tub until all the water has drained. Allow the bath to wash away any thoughts and patterns that will no longer serve you on your path.

As the water drains away, visualize and know that the negative energies now in the water are going into the Earth to be grounded.

Rise up out of the tub and do a self-blessing:

Anoint each area of your body with the sacred water, while saying out loud:

> *'Blessed be my mind that learns the way of the witch.*
>
> *Blessed be my eyes that have seen this day.*
>
> *Blessed be my lips that utter your names and keep your secrets.*
>
> *Blessed be my breasts formed in strength and beauty.*
>
> *Blessed be my womb for being the holy grail, cauldron and keeper of the mysteries.*
>
> *Blessed be my knees that shall kneel at my altar.*
>
> *Blessed be my feet that help me walk this path.'*

Pour a glass of wine or green juice – your libation is *totally* your call – to SHE and HE, and then take a sip.

Dry yourself off; and when you're ready, clean up the bathroom and take the libation offering outside to return it to the Earth (or pour it into a pot plant if you're a modern, urban witch).

The rite is ended.

So mote it be!

⁓ꙮ⁓

Opening Circle

Visualize yourself entering a circle of witches.

The air is thick with the smoke of burning mugwort – a cleansing herb I love to use for smudging. There's a fire burning, with flames licking at broken tree branches; and around it, women are gathered.

Come join us.

Take a look around the circle, and let your eyes meet the eyes of the women that are gathered with you. You may recognize some of them… or you may not.

They may be from this lifetime, or they may not.

One sister is chanting the various names given to the Mother God: *'Isis, Astarte, Diana, Hecate, Demeter, Kali, Inanna'* over and over, from deep down in her womb.

It feels ancient and timeless.

You are *home*.

∽ THE INVOCATION ぐ

Close your eyes. Take a deep breath. Relax your hands, palms face up, and be open to receive. As I call in each of the quarters (directions), turn to face that direction: we'll be going clockwise.

First, I turn to the East, and the element of Air. I invite you to blow out the old and bring in the new. Help us to allow the winds of change and not resist them.

Hail and welcome.

Next, to the South, and the element of Fire. I invite you to burn away regrets, ignite a fire of passion and desire, and be the flame that ignites the light of others when plunged into darkness.

Hail and welcome.

Next to the West, and the element of Water. I invite you to cleanse us, quench our thirst, nourish us, allow us to explore the ebb and flow of our emotions, and purify our thoughts.

Hail and welcome.

Finally, to the North, and the element of Earth. Hold us and support us as we grow strong roots so that we can rise.

Hail and welcome.

Mumma Earth, Father Sky, Grandmumma Moon, Grandfather Sun, Star Nations and the mysteries that lie in between – be with us, support us and guide us in our circle.

Ancestors, witches and wise women who've gone before us, please join us, sit with us and guide us in the circle.

SHE, divine feminine, lady of all that is, I ask for your presence and your blessing. Please clear the space of any heavy energy; and fill it with love, healing and truth.

SHE, I ask for you to work through me, to work through us, and to make sure we hear and feel what we need the most as we experience this circle, this book and our path together.

So mote it be.

༄

Regardless of where you are in the world, we are holding sacred and courageous space together. And FYI: the stronger the container, the stronger the magic.

Women have been doing this for thousands of years, gathering together, holding space – keeping and holding mysteries and secrets beyond time and space, because this is what witches do.

Courageous and wild witch – that's you, BTW – thank you for showing up, for being here and above all, for being you.

I didn't decide

to become a witch.

I remembered

I was one.

Chapter 1

Wake the Witches

February 2016. I'm sitting in Café Gratitude, Venice Beach, with Dana Gillespie, creatrix of the period tracking app My Moontime, *and Holly Grigg-Spall, author of* Sweetening The Pill. *The three of us are joking about how we are the Holy Freakin' Trinity of modern-day witches, gathered around a bowl of super-healthy food in a hipster part of LA.*

The three of us do women's work.

We talk about vaginas, wombs, periods and pussy power – loudly, and in public.

We do the work that the women who've gone before us would have been persecuted and killed for.

While the witch hunts no longer result in death (at least not in LA), all three of us still get trolled for it. Holly's been told to watch out for death threats because of the tireless work she does to bring attention to the detrimental effects that the contraceptive pill has on women's health and wellbeing.

Dana has been questioned and called 'nuts' by other women in the field of fertility education because her work isn't consistent with their strict beliefs.

And me? I get called out for being 'too much'. I get called names, and have my body/sexuality/beliefs judged and assumed because of the work I share in the world.

On *that* day in February, we talked about the popularity of the witch, and that now Instagram-famous quote *'We are the granddaughters of the witches you could not burn.'* Dana laughed and said, *'Forget that slogan! I'm the witch you DID burn, over and over, and I'm back, bitches!'*

We cackled; and as I stirred my beet and kale juice with an eco-friendly straw, the truth of that statement beat like a drum – ancient and familiar – deep down in my womb.

You see, I carry the wounds and scars of lifetimes of being burned and persecuted. It shows up as shame, fear, guilt and anxiety (and another gazillion variations on that theme).

I bet you feel it too.

That's why – despite the fear and trepidation I'd been feeling about writing this book – as I sat in Café Gratitude with my womb witches, I declared, *'Yes, we ARE back; and this time we're taking back our power. It's time to wake the witches!'* There were no fanfares, marching bands or big applause: just pussy-deep truth.

Fast forward to May 2016. I'm standing on sacred SHE landscape in Malta, an island in the Mediterranean sea, with eight women who each heard and responded to The Call. That Call went out in the form of an invitation to my email list to join me in a SHE Power Temple on this sacred island. It was an invitation to wake the witch, with no plan – just a gathering of hearts and wombs to join in ceremony and remember.

Together, we make nine.

It's a full moon. a fierce and powerful full moon. It's a moon under which all of our menstrual cycles have synced, despite us only being together for three days.

In circle, with bare feet, open hearts and wide arms, I invite these women to repeat after me:

'I call back my power. NOW.'

We repeat it three times without prompting – because when women gather in this way, prompting is very rarely needed. Then we take each other's hands and chant:

'WE call back our power. Now.'

It's visceral and bone-deep.

It's a calling-up and a calling-in of the ancient feminine wisdom and power that's held in the Earth beneath our feet. Where SHE – the Mother God, Goddess, the divine feminine – has been pushed down, suppressed, trodden on and kept in exile.

Together, in circle, under that full Flower Moon, we *dared* to call back our power. We did it for ourselves – for you, for me, for every woman who went before us and for every women who's yet to come.

It was the most powerful evocation I'd ever experienced.

And looking into each of those women's eyes, I saw my own reflection.

I saw women who were mothers. Women who were writers and artists. Women who, in their daily lives, were entrepreneurs and medicine keepers.

I saw women who all dared to show up in circle: fierce, vulnerable, strong, raw, soft and open to walking their own edges. Women who, over those three days, gathered for shared stories, magic making, unravelling and truth-telling messiness together.

I saw Mumma Earth.

I saw the Mother God.

I saw the Ancients.

I saw all the women who'd gone before.

I saw all the women who've yet to come.

I saw your reflection too.

And it was under THAT full moon, in ceremony with THOSE women, on THAT sacred land, that I truly claimed my title as a powerful-beyond-measure witch…

… Despite being a third-generation witch.

… Despite having re-initiated myself into the craft by immersing myself naked in the White Spring that bubbles in the belly of Glastonbury Tor.

… Despite experiencing the full force and magic of Mumma Nature and her cycles of death and rebirth (over and over again).

… And despite having been to countless group rituals and Sabbat celebrations (as well as hosting many solo).

Why?

Well, there was a time when I'd have said that terms and titles didn't matter. And in most circumstances, I still believe that to be true.

But when it comes to the word 'witch'? It matters.

It matters A LOT.

Being a witch is remembering.

It's the GREAT remembering.

It's the remembering of who you were before you forgot.

And then it's the lifelong job/journey/quest/adventure of reconnecting – over and over again – to your forgotten knowing.

I invite you to start reconnecting with that forgotten knowing here.

The Witch

In each and every woman, there is a creature.

She is wild, and she's a reflection of Nature.

She's a powerful force.

She's a power source.

She's passionate, creative, deeply intuitive and has a knowing that's older than time itself.

And that creature's name?

The witch.

The witch is often painted as an ugly, scary woman who does bad things, but this is NOT the truth.

She's often seen as a spell caster, a weaver of dark arts and someone who creates hexes and curses. And, hmm, this is SOMETIMES the truth.

Rarely, however, is the witch seen as a wise woman, a power source and a force of Nature.

Yet this is ACTUALLY the truth.

Forget everything you've ever been told about witches.

Forget the images of the dark, the hag-like or the forbidden. Forget the three witches in Shakespeare's *Macbeth*. Forget black candles, broomsticks, poison, evil incantations, Satan and cauldrons – and let me instead tell you a different story.

It's a story where you no longer fear the word witch.

A story where you discover that the fear you've experienced has been part of a 3,000+ year-old patriarchal plan to keep you from your own innate feminine power.

A story where you're invited to reclaim the word witch.

To own it.

Fully.

And more importantly, you're invited to own the power that belongs to that word.

What Is a Witch?

A witch is an unapologetic woman.

She alchemizes experiences and emotions.

She's a woman with power, agency and sovereignty... and she has it on HER terms.

She creates and manifests.

She is self-sourced.

She freely communes with Nature/Spirit/God/dess/choose-your-own-semantics without needing a go-between.

Being a witch is being a woman in her power.

It's being someone who trusts her inner authority, and doesn't look outside herself for validation and/or approval. It's being someone who uses her own personal magic to navigate and negotiate the environment she currently finds herself in.

The Call

I've talked about The Call already a little in this chapter. It's that powerful pull you feel – that invitation-bordering-on-a-command – from something at once bigger than you are, and deep within your own heart.

The Call can take different forms for different women. For you, it might look like:

- A need to read ALL the books on spellcraft
- A need to fight for the rights of the whales
- A need to fight for Mumma Earth or some other worthy cause close to your heart

Or it might have no form at all – just a really uncomfy feeling.

Regardless, because the witch has been underground for so long, The Call that you're currently experiencing probably feels painful. That's not surprising: you're being asked to navigate some unexplored terrain in your life, and to deliberately wake and cultivate the witch within yourself so that she can reach her fullest potential.

Let me make this super-clear: you don't need to be a Wiccan or a Pagan to be a witch.

In fact, you don't even need to know what either of these terms mean. All you need is a deep sense of knowing who you are underneath all the noise, labels and societal messaging.

That's why your roots, and the practices and traditions that accompany them, are the best place to start waking the witch within you.

Me? I'm a Gypsy, a yogini and a shamana – so, y'know, go figure. Essentially, I'm a Gypsy witch. My maternal lineage is Irish Traveller, and my paternal line is Roma.

Both of my nannas used herbs, teas, tinctures, oils and potions to manifest, heal and create good luck for our families, and for the families in our community.

Both of them were gifted with seer-like vision; and through dreams, intuitive knowing, tarot cards and scrying, they could predict the birth and the gender of babies. They'd also foresee family dramas that had yet to occur, and they'd know when financial scarcity was imminent (at which point, my uncles would be sent out to find extra work).

My Roma nanna, however, had a touch of the dark. She was locally renowned for her ability to throw a curse (some ex-boyfriends have said that I, too, have the same ability. I will neither confirm nor deny this. Ahem.). And although, for many, the idea of being a Gypsy conjures up super-romantic images of pretty painted wagons, headscarves and hoop earrings, the reality of Gypsy life is...well, NOT that.

When telling the stories of the witches who've gone before, we speak often of their persecution. We go back into history, and we discuss the witch trials in both Europe and America (read more about this on pages 66–70).

But for both the Roma and Travellers alike, persecution is still very much a real, everyday experience. My Roma nanna, who wore her entire wealth as gold jewellery all at once around her neck and in her ears, would tell me repeatedly, *'Don't trust no gadje! Never trust them, d'ya hear?'*

The persecution and mistrust was, and is, real.

That's why I know that both nannas would be furious at me for writing this book.

For sharing our secrets and for exposing myself as a witch.

And my mumma?

Well, *she'd* go batshit crazy.

You see, my mumma was an epic seer and dreamer. She'd have visions and insights and downloads in her dreamtime. (I only found this out in the last few months of her life, when she gave me her dream diary, filled with symbols and signs that I will probably spend the rest of my life decoding.)

Yet she chose to shun her gift and her Gypsy witch connection for most of her living years, because of the ever-present fear of being persecuted.

Honestly? My mumma lived in fear of almost everything.

She feared the dark, flying, driving, spiders and people with power. She feared life itself on most days; and her life became small and unfulfilled because of it.

When I decided to re-initiate myself as a witch by immersing myself in the White Spring in Glastonbury (read about that on page 54) she was terrified I'd *actually* tell people.

That I'd say out loud, 'I'm a witch'.

That her friends would find out.

That people wouldn't employ me.

That people wouldn't talk to me.

She'd hush me if I spoke too loudly about it. Even in the house.

But guess what?

That fear, the hiding in the shadows, the always feeling like you have to live life as an outsider on the outskirts of society?

It stops with me.

That was how it was for them, and I get why they were scared. Of course I do. But that's even more reason for me to declare:

'This is *my* time. This is *my* hour.

No more hiding in the shadows.

No more trying to find a different, more user-friendly word for what it is that I am.

I'm a witch.

I'm a powerful woman.

I'm a sacred source.

A force.

Of Nature.'

If you're reading this, if you picked up this book, then it's your time too.

It's time to wake the witches.

You are a woman rooting.

A woman remembering.

A witch waking.

This Is Witch Work

Calling yourself a witch at this moment in history is a BIG deal.

Our way of being as women has been persecuted for millennia. The word 'witch' has been vilified and slung around as an insult. So it's no wonder that we, as women, hold back our power, hush our voices and stay small because we've been told that being powerful is unsafe.

Our work, the work of the witch, is to make it safe to be powerful again.

Being powerful in the face of thousands of years of patriarchal expectations and conditioning means going against so many of the things you've been taught, right?

And yet... the power to shape events, to change things up and make things happen flows naturally through you. Your biology is honed and optimized to wield that power and use it for good.

It's your birthright as a woman.

This is witch work.

The thing is, so many of us have grown really good at playing the roles we've been offered up as women in the world.

The award for best actress? It goes to...ALL OF US.

The problem? I don't know about you, but when I've played these roles (and I've played *many* of them in the past), I've always found myself feeling a combination of unfulfilled/hungry/displeased/restless.

And if you feel that restlessness too? That's the unexpressed part of you.

Over time, that part of you starts to *scream* inside.

The scream becomes deafening. All-consuming.

For some it shows up as pain and dis-ease in the body. For others it'll be depression and/or anxiety.

You may use food/drink/shopping/drugs to numb it.

At first, you'll probably push it down.

And in pushing down the scream, you'll go one of two ways. You'll either become despondent and submissive to life, or you'll become aggressive and/or hardened – taking on predominantly masculine traits to survive.

My mumma? She took the submissive role. She dimmed her own light so that others could shine. She sought the permission of others daily, and always looked outside herself for validation.

She didn't trust herself. She didn't dare.

Me, on the other hand? I took the other role.

I totally disconnected from my female body. I lived my life from the neck up, operating and making decisions from my head. I lived life like a dude because that option seemed much easier than having to deal with being a woman who was never seen or heard.

(That disconnection from my female body and her cyclic nature led to PCOS and endometriosis. I speak about this experience in detail in my book *Love Your Lady Landscape*. So FYI, it was NOT the easier option.)

Pushing down the scream is what we're dealing with here. And it's not exclusive to my mumma and me: it's a basic reality for so many women in the western world.

Recognize it in your body. Recognize it in your being, because it's time to stop pushing it down. It's time to start letting it all be seen and felt. FULLY.

This is witch work.

How do we dare to express our fullness?

We must bring it ALL.

Rage AND laughter.

Beauty AND strength.

Fierceness AND grace.

Vulnerability AND force.

Compassion AND passion.

And guess what? You don't need to be *less* of anything.

In fact, I invite you to be *more* of everything.

So many of us have an innate need to be liked and approved of. It's human nature, but it also means we've been conditioned (really bloody well) into making a thousand subtle compromises. It means we've become women who don't dare to live out our fullness. We make sure we're not 'too quiet', and make sure we're not 'too loud'.

I see it in myself.

I see it in the women I work with.

We never fully allow ourselves to go ALL THE WAY. We hold back, rein it in and tame our true nature in any given moment, just in case we get judged/shamed/accused based on who we are in THAT particular moment.

Women, this is NO way to live.

I repeat: this is NO WAY TO LIVE.

You can *never* claim back your power by being less of yourself, or by squeezing yourself tight enough to fit inside the narrow box marked '100% approved.'

Power can't come from being 'less than'. It just can't.

It can *only* come from expanding and growing and expressing yourself FULLY.

From daring to take up space.

Becoming *more* of everything.

This is witch work.

Women who are scared of the word 'witch' and all that it represents are also scared of their own power. And if that's true for you, that's okay. You've been taught to be scared.

You've been told that 'power corrupts'. The image you have right now of someone who seeks power is probably someone who's selfish and greedy. Someone who'll stop at nothing to get that power, even if it's at someone else's expense, right?

And it's true. This version of power is definitely one to be wary of.

But like 'witch', 'bitch', 'cunt' and 'menstruation', 'power' is NOT the dirty word we've been taught it is.

We absolutely need to embrace, rather than reject, the idea of power in order to claim our fullness and our true expression in the world as women.

So… what if there was a definition of power that felt good? One that didn't feel dirty, selfish or sleazy?

To get to that definition, you'd have to:

… Learn that ideas like selfishness, manipulation and greed are what corrupts, NOT power.

… Trust your own, feminine inner authority to nurture you and those around you.

… Realize that your positive intentions grow stronger when you're more powerful, not weaker.

This is witch work.

The Tower card in the tarot is associated with change. It's like the goddess Kali Ma: it represents burning down what's no longer necessary.

Are you ready to walk into the fire? Again?

Witch work means that you have to burn over and over. All the bloody time.

It means having to burn up the stories you've been told in order to keep you tame and compliant.

It means unlocking the shackles and undoing the ties that have bound you.

You can't wait until you feel strong enough or brave enough before you take a stand or take a risk. Why? Because while you're in your cage, you stay tame.

You can only find your power when you plug yourself back into the motherboard. When your feet touch Mumma Earth, and your womb and heart connect with her.

When you connect with SHE.

You find and claim your power when you interact daily with a world that's in need. When you practise being the most powerful being you can be.

It might feel that there's so much work to do; but actually, it's the *only* work there is to do. So many of us spend our entire lives wondering, 'What's our passion? What's our purpose? What do we have to do?'

What we have to do is THIS.

Witch work.

FYI: that's the work you *know* you're here to do.

This is witch work.

Just so you know, to do this work, you need to get comfy with a lot more discomfort than most people are willing to put up with.

You have to be willing to:

- Feel. Everything. Joy, pain, fear, anger, distress. You have to be willing to feel it all. To feel the whole freakin' world.

- Disappoint people in order to be your true self.

- Know that you are chained to nothing and no one.

- Breathe. Deeply. Right down deep into your womb.

- Find fierceness and healing and peace in those places of yourself that seem hard and closed off.

- Let the feminine parts of yourself lead the masculine. Don't get rid of the masculine (you'll need it!), but let the wild nature and chaos and softness of the feminine inform the harder edges of your soul.

- Love yourself. Even the most wild and crazy parts.

Don't be alarmed when you love yourself and those around you so hard that you're asked to enter a new level of raw and intimate reality. It's intense and it's powerful, but *damn*, it's so good and worth it.

It's a place that's a magnet for beauty and connection.

A place you dream of.

A place you *know* is yours.

Know that this place is yours.

THIS is witch work.

Take back
the term witch
and the power
that belongs to it.

Chapter 2

Which Witch Is Which?

Roots, Traditions and Walking The Path

'A witch is a wise woman aligned with the Earth, a healer. It's a word that demands destigmatization at this crucial time in the planet's history when we desperately need the medicine of the feminine to rise and rebalance humanity and the Earth.'

– SARAH DURHAM WILSON

Being a witch – and witchcraft itself – comes in many, many different forms and flavours.

For some, being a witch is a sacred and spiritual practice. For others it's a political statement, a way of life or a belief system. And yet to others, being a witch is their religion.

Some forms of witchcraft are based on historical evidence, while others arise from archaeological and anthropological discoveries. Some are passed down through cultural practices, from mumma to daughter, grandmother to granddaughter, generation to generation. Others are based on oral traditions passed down through families, communities or cultures.

Some of the more Neo-Pagan traditions – specifically ones like Alexandrian and Gardnerian, which were created by men – work on levels of hierarchical training. In these traditions, you have to learn and demonstrate within a coven before being initiated by a high priest or priestess in order to receive a title. Others only worship the Goddess and completely disregard a male god.

Me? Well, I'm not Wiccan, but some of the people I've studied with are.

Some of my practices are infused with a Wiccan flavour – specifically, with the work of Doreen Valiente (read more about her on page 32). However, they're also steeped in my family traditions, and in other traditions I've explored. My spiritual orientation is eclectic, and what I share draws upon all the teachings that have formed my magical relationship with reality. My style of magical working – and my relationship with magic in general – is intuitive.

Essentially, I'm a witch of the old ways.

And when I say 'old ways', I mean The REALLY old ways – back when witchcraft was *wiccecraeft* (also spelled *wiccecraefte*, *wicchecrafte*, *witchcraft*). That word literally meant the *Craft* – as in the art or skill of the *wicce* (pronounced *wit-cha*).

The *wicce* was the cunning woman, the healer, the wise one of a tribe or community who could 'bend and shape'. Yep, she was a worker of magic who was so attuned to her intuitive relationship with herself that she could bend the energies of nature to promote healing, growth and new life. She'd shape her life and the lives of her community to be harmonious with Mumma Nature.

She trusted and worshipped source, the Goddess, SHE – and she knew that she herself was a direct reflection of SHE.

Now that's *my* kind of witchcraft.

Which Way Do You Witch?

There are so many traditions of witchcraft and so many different types of witches. In fact, there are far too many to share here; but in the following pages, I've listed some of the more popular hereditary traditions and Neo-Pagan forms of witchcraft.

This isn't a definitive list, and I'm not suggesting that you have to pick one. Nor am I here to tell you whether one of them is right or wrong. Instead, I wanted to share a 'finger pinch' of what's available for you to explore further.

They're in alphabetical order, so if you're looking for a specific tradition, it should be easy to find.

Alexandrian Witch

The Alexandrian covens were founded in England during the 1960s by Alexander Sanders, self-proclaimed 'King of the Witches'.

An offshoot of Gardnerian witchcraft, Alexandrian witchcraft focuses strongly on training. It emphasizes areas that are more generally associated with ceremonial magic, such as Qabalah and Angelic Magic.

A typical Alexandrian coven has a hierarchical structure, and generally comes together weekly in meetings called 'circles'. At the very least, they'll meet on full moons, new moons and Sabbats. Their rituals are usually done skyclad (naked).

Most Alexandrian covens will allow a non-initiate to attend their circles, usually as a 'beginner' who undergoes basic training in circle craft before being accepted for the first-degree initiation.

Alexandrian Wicca uses essentially the same tools and rituals as Gardnerian Wicca, although in some cases, it uses the tools differently and adapts the rituals. It also frequently changes the names of deities and the guardians of the quarters.

In some ways, the differences are merely cosmetic; but in others, there are fundamental differences in philosophy.

Appalachian 'Granny' Tradition Witch

This tradition dates back to the first Scottish and Irish settlers of the Appalachian Mountains in the 1700s, who brought with them their magical traditions of the 'old ways'.

The Appalachian settlers blended their own traditions with the local tradition of the Cherokee tribes, creating a combination of local herbal folk remedies and charms, faith healing, storytelling and magic.

The term 'Granny Tradition' is due to the prominent role that older women play in the mountain communities.

However, today 'Granny' Witches often call themselves 'Doctor Witches' or 'Water Witches', depending upon whether they're more gifted in healing and midwifery, or in dowsing for water, ley lines and energy vortexes.

Asatru and Followers of the Northern Tradition

Asatru is a term that means 'loyalty to the Aesir (a group of Norse Gods)'. It's a religion associated with Norse Heathenism (the contemporary revival of historical Germanic Paganism), and is based on the surviving historical records of the Norse Pagan religions.

Asatru stays close to the original religion of the Norse people; and in modern Scandinavia it's often called 'Forn Siðr' or the 'Ancient Way'. In fact, in Iceland, it's a recognized state religion.

The origins of Asatru are genuinely ancient, and it recognizes many gods and goddesses, including:

- **Thor and his mighty hammer:** Thor controls the storms, with thunder being the sound of his chariot, and rain being his way of allowing crops to prosper.

- **Odin:** the god who gifted us with a divine nature. He's the one-eyed god, who traded his eye for wisdom, then hung on the World Tree to learn the mysteries of magic and the runes.

- **Freya:** the goddess who wears a sacred necklace and rides a cat-drawn chariot. She's the goddess of love and beauty, but she's also a fierce goddess of battle.

- **Frigg:** Odin's wife, who shares in his leadership of the gods.

- **Skadi:** a goddess of strong independence, and patron of hunting and skiing.

Asatru practitioners seek the old mysteries of the land, and honour the Landvættir (land spirits) who dwell in the trees, rocks, land and waters. They also honour their ancestors: both those who've gone to the other worlds, and those – such as the Disir – who remain connected to Middle Earth (this physical world) in order to watch over and protect their family.

Bruja or Curandera

'Bruja' is the Spanish word for 'witch'; and 'Curandera' means 'healer' in Spanish.

Both words are used to describe the witches, healers and medicine workers of a specific Hispanic folk-healing tradition that continues today in a variety of forms in the USA and Latin America (including Mexico).

Like many forms of witchcraft and healing, Curanderismo (the path of the Curandera) and Brujeria (the tradition of the Bruja) were both suppressed for a long time. This suppression started with the Spanish conquistadors, who imposed their cultural values on indigenous populations; but there's been a recent resurgence amongst young Latina and Hispanic women.

The magical workings and practices of each tradition can include ritual, cleansings, energy work, spirit contact, divination, honouring the Earth, working closely with nature and a *lot* of prayer.

Practitioners also use a variety of objects including herbs, spices, eggs, lemons, limes, holy water, saints, crucifixes, prayer, candles, incense, oils and divination tools; and the rituals often invoke the help of the Catholic saints, folk saints, family members who've passed on or another spirit.

Celtic Witch

The Celtic path is really many traditions that fall under the general heading of 'Celtic'. It encompasses Druidism, Celtic Shamanism, Celtic Wicca or Witta and the Grail Religion.

Celtic witchcraft is primarily derived from the ancient pre-Christian Celtic religion of Gaul and the British Isles. As they're practiced today, most of the Celtic paths are part of the Neo-Pagan revival, focusing on nature and healing, with group and individual rituals that honour the Ancients and the Earth. Most are very eclectic, but hold true to the Celtic myths, deities, magic and rituals.

Celtic paths are some of the more popular traditions amongst Pagans in the British Isles. They work with the elements, the Ancient Ones and nature. Followers are usually healers who work with plants, stones, flowers, trees, the elemental people, the gnomes and the fairies.

Dianic Witch

Dianic witchcraft is a mixture of different traditions. Its primary focus is the Goddess, who is worshiped in her three aspects of Maiden, Mother and Crone.

Dianic witchcraft is a 'divine feminine tradition', so its covens are for women only. To an outside observer, it may appear as a single tradition, but actually it's really an intertwined group of traditions that have influenced each other over the centuries and millennia.

Most Dianic covens worship the Goddess exclusively (Diana and Artemis are the most common manifestations), and most today are still women-only.

Dianic rituals are eclectic: some are derived from the Gardnerian tradition, while others have been created anew. They emphasize rediscovering and reclaiming female power and divinity, consciousness-raising and combining politics with spirituality.

Z Budapest, badass witch, declared Dianic Witchcraft to be 'Wimmin's Religion'. She founded The Women's Spirituality Forum in 1986, and is dedicated to bringing Goddess and feminist consciousness to the mainstream.

Eclectic Witch

Eclectic witchcraft is an approach for individuals who want to pick and choose from many different traditions to create a personalized form of witchcraft that meets their individual needs and abilities.

Eclectic witches don't follow any particular religion or tradition. Instead, they study and learn from many different systems, and use what works best for them. They build a tailor-made religion or tradition for themselves from the ground up, rather than following an established tradition.

Practitioners' minds remain open and receptive to the knowledge, ideas, beliefs and methods that others practise. They adapt well to different situations, and create their own paths based on what they believe to be true and right at that time in their life.

In other words, simply put – they don't follow rules. Instead, they like to explore, make their own mistakes and take from their experiences to create their own rules and traditions.

Gardnerian Witch

Named after Gerald Gardner, this tradition enfolds elements of several ancient traditions. Because of its local origins, (Gardner practised in The New Forest, a few miles from me in the UK), it also incorporates the folklore and customs of English Paganism.

Gardnerian witches worship the Horned God and the Goddess of Nature. Generally, practitioners celebrate their rituals skyclad.

A high priest and high priestess lead each coven, emphasizing the leadership of the high priestess. The Gardnerian system marks spiritual progress using a series of initiatory rites, and is based on gender bi-polarity, which means that all things are divided into masculine/feminine opposites.

Green/Eco Witch

Green witchcraft (also known as Eco-witchcraft) is the practice of nature- and earth-based witchcraft.

An Eco witch draws on the folklore, folk religion and folk magic of ancient cultures such as the tree worship of Druids, the kitchen craft of Italian witches and the keeping of sacred groves in Gallic Paganism.

Green witches usually practise a traditional form of witchcraft in which they consult the Earth, trees, herbs, plants and flowers for their medicinal and magical value. They generally grow their own herbs or wildcraft (harvest plant food and medicine from its natural, or 'wild' habitat). They're generally very good at making herbal tinctures, potions and remedies.

Belief in deities depends on the individual witch, though many Green witches acknowledge an Earth Mother or a series of nature spirits as deities. The dead (both human and animal) and the Fey also play a large part in Green traditions.

A form of Green witchcraft known as *Green Wicca* was made popular by Ann Moura in her book *Green Witchcraft: Folk Magic, Fairy Lore and Herb Craft.*

Gypsy or Romani Shuvihani

The Romani tradition uses simple spells and rituals to harness the power of nature and of the elemental spirits that are all around us.

Evidence strongly demonstrates that Romani Gypsies actually originated in India and moved west, migrating through the Middle East into Europe.

Roma talents in divination and spellcraft have always been much in demand; and despite the Gypsy holocaust (which the Roma called 'The Devouring'), Romani shuvihani *still* maintain their magic.

The Romani word for wise woman, 'shuvihani', has much the same meaning as 'witch'. A shuvihani knows the rites and rituals for occasions such as weddings and baby blessings, as well as how to use herbs and divination for spells.

Hedge Witch

Hedge craft is a path that is somewhat shamanic in nature. Practitioners are sometimes simply referred to as 'wise women', because they practise an Earth-based spirituality.

In older times a 'hedge' signified the boundary of the village. In the term 'hedge craft', it represents the boundary that exists between this world and the spiritual realm.

Hedge witches are the ones who journey into the other world. They can, in this capacity, be very powerful midwives and herbal healers. They are also said to be night travellers or walkers on the wind. Their main function is to mediate between the spirits and people in the physical realm.

Some claim that hedge craft is the continuation of the practices of the ancient cunning folk and wise-women, while others say that it's a modern tradition.

Either way, a bird of one kind or another is usually associated with hedge witches, most commonly a raven or a goose.

Hereditary Witch

The term 'hereditary witch' is given to witches who've inherited their magic gifts through their bloodline.

Hereditary witches are usually born to a magical family, and begin their journey very early in their life, using the gifts handed down through the generations.

These traditions are often not recorded, except perhaps in grimoires and Books of Shadows (read more about these on page 150), which are passed down but very highly protected.

Usually, however, a hereditary witch relies primarily on oral and physical teachings from her family. Each family has its own unique traditions, and most will stick together as family units rather than create covens.

Hoodoo Witch

Hoodoo, Conjure and Rootwork are all terms used to describe the practices of African American and Native American folk medicine and magic.

Hoodoo is a nature-based healing tradition that consists of a large body of African folkloric practices and beliefs, mixed together with Native American botanical knowledge and European folklore. It should not be confused with Voodoo, which is a religion.

Sticks, Stones, Roots and Bones is more than the name of my favourite book on Hoodoo written by Stephanie Rose Bird. It's also a description of the basic ingredients used in a Hoodoo mojo bag (a personal talisman worn or carried to bring love, prosperity, protection or luck. Find out how to make your own on page 170.)

Hoodoo attributes magical properties to herbs, roots, minerals, animal parts and the personal possessions and bodily fluids of people; and uses each of these things in its magical workings.

Kitchen Witch

The kitchen witch is super-practical and works predominantly with the elements, the Ancient Ones and nature.

A kitchen witch is usually a healer, and someone who's respected in her community. Once she's past menopause, she tends to take on a 'Wise Woman' role, as her abundance of knowledge is respected, admired and revered.

The kitchen witch works with plants, stones, flowers, trees, fairies and gnomes; but above all, she performs her magic in the kitchen. She has Goddess-given talents for food crafting and making potions and herbal remedies. She also has natural instincts for protecting her hearth and home.

This witch doesn't need ceremonial tools: she uses the same knife to chop carrots for soup and to prepare herbs for a spell or tincture. If you were ever going to give my nanna a 'witch' label, THIS would be it!

Shamana/Shamanka

A shamana is a female shaman or medicine woman whose practices are drawn from those of shamans in traditional Pagan cultures throughout the world.

While many witches focus solely on the craft of the witch through spells and rituals, the mysteries of witchcraft are very shamanic. A shamana (sometimes called 'shamanka') combines the roles of healer, herbalist, priestess, diviner, magician and teacher. She works deeply with the spirits and plants to heal all levels of their being.

Shamanas typically enter into a trance state or other altered state of consciousness through drumming, dancing and using teacher plants during a ritual or ceremony.

Shamanic witchcraft emphasizes serving the wider community through rituals, herbalism, spellcraft, healings, counselling, rites of passage, handfastings (a specific form of marriage), mystery initiations, etc.

Stregheria

Stregheria is native Italian witchcraft, which is also called La Vecchia Religione. *Stregheria is a nature-based religion: its followers worship the forces of nature, personified as gods and goddesses.*

The modern Stregheria tradition taught by Raven Grimassi in the book *Ways of the Strega* derives from a magical practice that occurred in the 14th century, shared by a Tuscan wise woman called Aradia.

This doesn't mean that Italian witchcraft began in the 14th century, however. Aradia's tradition was a revival of the Old Ways, and included the secrets of the Earth, the moon and the stars.

When the persecution of peasants and witches in Italy began, however, the tradition split. Each group was entrusted with one section of the mysteries.

- **The *Fanarra*:** the Keepers of the Earth Mysteries kept the secrets of ley lines and the forces of the Earth.

- **The *Janarra*:** the Keepers of the Lunar Mysteries were entrusted with the mysteries of the energy and powers of la Luna (the moon).

- **The *Tanarra*:** the Keepers of the Stellar Mysteries hold the magic and knowledge of star forces.

Common to all three traditions in the modern day are the arts of herbalism, divination, magic, ritual and other aspects associated with the old pre-Christian ways.

Thelema Witch

Thelema is a Greek word meaning 'will' or 'intention'. It's also the name of a spiritual philosophy developed in the early part of the 20th century by an Englishman named Aleister Crowley.

Crowley was a poet, author, mountaineer, magician and member of the occult society known as the Hermetic Order of the Golden Dawn.

He coined the term 'magick', which he defined as 'the Science and Art of causing Change to occur in conformity with Will'. He spelled the word magic with a 'k' at the end to set the spiritual discipline of magick apart from sleight-of-hand tricks and stage magic.

A Thelemic ritual (i.e. 'magick') is a pre-determined series of actions that's designed to accomplish a given purpose. It might include gestures, chants, reciting invocations, visualizations, meditation, etc.

A practitioner often performs spells and rituals in either a sacred grove or outdoor location, or in an indoor space set up as a temple; and can do so alone or as part of a group.

Practitioners may also use candles, incense, and magical implements such as a wand, cup, dagger and pentacle, depending on the requirements of their particular ritual. All of these elements combine to imprint the practitioner's desired change in their own consciousness.

Traditional Witch

A traditional witch is one who's interested in the old (pre-Christian) ways. They often follow history and the arts to build a foundation for their craft.

Traditional witches are less inclined to participate in worshipping the Goddess or gods, preferring to work predominantly with the spirit world and the landscape. They will often also call on their ancestors or land spirits to support them in their magical workings.

Traditional Witches tend to work with moon cycles, planetary symbols and cycles, rune symbols and herbs. They honour both the land and their ancestors. Traditional Witches work with both the dark and the light. They perform banishing and repelling spells, and do not follow the threefold law or the Wiccan Rede, (just to be super-clear, Traditional Witchcraft is *not* Wicca). However, they carefully consider any magic they intend to perform and take responsibility for it, whether it's healing, a hex or banishing spells.

Traditional witches believe in three worlds.

- **The Under World**: populated by those who've died, either awaiting reincarnation or choosing not to pass on (and those who can't ascend).

- **The Middle World**: the here and now.

- **The Upper World**: populated by spirits/souls who've ascended, and no longer need their bodies, or who were never bonded to a physical form/body to begin with.

What About Wicca?

Modern witchcraft, specifically Wicca, owes much of its origins to Gerald Gardner (the Englishman responsible for Gardnerian Witchcraft).

In 1939, Gardner claimed to have been initiated into a traditional Witchcraft coven in the New Forest, UK, by its high priestess, Dorothy Clutterbuck. Based on this, he began to write his own interpretations of ancient Pagan Witchcraft; and it was from his teachings – especially his 1954 book *Witchcraft Today* – that the tradition of Wicca established itself.

Doreen Valiente and the Beyoncé-fication of Wicca

During the first part of Gardner's life, he travelled for many years in the Far East, observing indigenous people and their spiritual beliefs. The Wiccan tradition reflects many of the teachings and experiences Gardner was exposed to as he travelled.

In fact, many people questioned whether he was ever *really* initiated by a coven; or whether he was instead simply heavily influenced by his experiences and the ancient esoteric and ceremonial documents that he read.

Regardless: many people (including me) credit high priestess Doreen Valiente for the emphasis that Wicca puts on the Goddess. For me, Valiente was one of *the* most important figures in Wicca. She wrote down much of its ritual and worship; and she played an integral part in lifting the legal ban on witchcraft on 29 July 1951, which had been in place for over two centuries at that point.

Gardner interpreted the ancient rites and rituals, but Valiente was basically the Beyoncé of her time. She was the author of the *Charge of the Goddess*, a poetic invocation of the Goddess that is used in almost all Wiccan and many other Pagan ceremonies across the world today. She also put flesh on the bones of the written witch lore that Gardner showed her, and gave the modern Craft a logical (and lyrical) framework.

This allowed it to be easily passed on through initiation. And honestly? I believe that her Beyoncé-fication of Wicca is the reason it spread so widely and rapidly, and that it continues to expand across the world today.

Doreen was a *badass*.

So, What is Wicca Exactly?

Wicca is a recognized modern religion, based on ancient witchcraft traditions. It's a nature-based religion that worships an 'ultimate life force' from which it believes that the male and female aspects of life – the God and Goddess – began.

In Wicca, the Divine, God or Goddess (depending on who you speak to) can have different names. Wicca contains references to different goddesses and gods from other theological systems and pantheons: Hindu, Egyptian, Buddhist, ancient Greek, Sumerian, and even Christian. The tradition celebrates seasonal holidays like the equinoxes and solstices in a cycle that's known as the Wheel of the Year.

There are two basic codes by which Wiccans live:

- **The Wiccan Rede**: this states, 'An Ye Harm None, Do What Ye Will'. This means a Wiccan is free to use her magic as long as it doesn't harm anyone.

- **The Threefold Law**: this states that any good you do will return to you threefold in this lifetime. Likewise, any harm you do will return to you threefold as well.

Obviously, there's a LOT more to Wicca and to *all* the traditions than I've been able to share here. What should be super-clear, however, is how similar they all are.

For the most part, witchcraft – regardless of specific tradition – is the traditional folk magic/healing/medicine of the indigenous people; and a witch is the wise person/healer/medicine woman who shares it. The newer traditions, like those created by Crowley, Gardner and Alexander, are much more structured in their approach; but they still all have nature and the elements at their core.

Each witch's practice will be deeply personal: a combination of beliefs that they've learned along their own journey. Some witches will identify with a religion like Wicca, and some won't. Some will like and need the structure of a tradition like Gardnerian witchcraft, while others will prefer to work alone and pave their own path.

So, After All That, What Exactly Is a Witch?

There *is* NO one-size-fits-all answer, and thank the Goddess for that, right?

Every woman is a witch, regardless of whether she knows it or not.

Why? Because she's cyclic, she's powerful and she can embrace nature to heal herself AND her community.

In other words: she IS magic.

But I also know that buying a mini-cauldron from eBay and chanting a spell doesn't make you a witch. Nor does collecting titles or degrees, or completing initiations either.

Being a witch isn't about what you *do*. It's not spells, rituals and ceremony: it's the stance you take in life.

It's who you are at your source.

I don't call my witchcraft by any particular name, because it's a mashup of everything I am culturally, and everything I've learned, loved and implemented from the witches, wise women and healers that I've met along the way.

I've read witch books forever. Some I've loved, others I've laughed at and some have actually really scared me.

My litmus test for all of this?

I judge nothing.

I try most things.

I ask myself, 'Does this feel right?'

I check in with my heart, my gut and my womb, and I let my intuition guide me.

Don't trust all the books. Don't even trust this book – or trust me, either. Trust yourself.

I'm a witch who works *with* roots and *from her* roots.

I'm a Witch

'I am a witch, by which I mean that I am somebody who believes that the Earth is sacred; and that women and women's bodies are an expression of that sacred being.'
— STARHAWK

I'm a witch who casts spells, and howls under big full moons.

I'm a witch who celebrates the Sabbats and dances the spiral.

I'm a witch who has studied the paths of the wise witches who've been before: Sybil Leek, Marie Laveau, Doreen Valiente, Starhawk – I thank you and love you.

I'm a witch who trusts the wisdom of her fierce and feminine soul.

I'm a witch who sat in my nanna's aproned lap as she picked herbs and whispered incantations over freshly made tinctures.

I'm a witch who works *with* roots and *from her* roots.

I'm a witch who can call up power from the Earth, and call down power from the moon.

I'm a witch who works with Mumma Nature and her cycles to create and manifest life, dreams and wishes into being.

I'm a witch who has been burned with shame, who burns with passion, and who – at another time, in another place – would have been burned at the stake.

Which witch are you?

Walking Your Path

Witchcraft today is being built upon the idea that the Western world has lost, buried, suppressed and corrupted the old traditions of those who've gone before. Women like you and me are now waking up, remembering and attempting to rediscover those traditions and make them relevant again in the world we currently live in.

But, how, in a world where we – as woman – have been made to feel separate from ourselves, from each other and from the landscape around us, do we hear what the land, the Goddess, source, SHE, is telling us?

Here's what I do…

Get still – ideally in nature

Honour and cherish the power of stillness. You don't have to label it as meditation or mindfulness: just literally be quiet and let yourself, your mind and your nervous system be still. Drop below the chatter and doing-ness of life, and begin to understand who you are, who you *really* are.

If you can be still in nature, even better.

It's in the stillness that you'll hear the whispers: the whispers of source, of SHE, of nature, of the trees and of the flowers.

In the natural world, it's easier to remember who you are.

If you trace your ancestors back, you'll see that they lived in harmony with the cycles of nature. The problem is that we've been separated from nature; and now, the genetic bloodline that lives inside of you is urging you to take time to reconnect. It's urging you to put your back up against a tree, place your palms on the trunk and be still.

Follow your urges.

Tell the truth

Your soul loves the truth, so take time to begin to understand what *your* truth is. (And know that you can only do this in stillness!)

Often, when you're running around and 'doing' all the time, it's hard to know what you actually feel. Sometimes you think that you *should* be having fun, or *should* be sad, or should, should, should…

Forget the 'should'! What's your truth?

Listen to your body.

Your body will tell you *your* truth. If you start talking to someone and you get a headache, it *could* be dehydration. OR it could be your body telling you this person isn't okay, or that this conversation is whack and it isn't working for you.

This is how you start to trust yourself and your intuition – by telling yourself the truth. Tune in at every moment.

Pick up a crystal, or an item of jewellery or clothing. Does your energy go up, or does it go down? Start to practise this with people, places and items. Tune in to each thing, and then tell yourself the truth.

The more you lie to yourself, the harder it is to step into your power as a witch.

Don't lie to yourself.

Step beyond fear

This is challenging, especially when you're in the middle of fear.

But start by naming the fear, because a fear named is a fear tamed.

Then turn that fear around.

My biggest fear has always been: 'I'm afraid they'll reject me if I speak my truth.'

Naming that out loud was huge for me. But naming it and then turning it around? That was a *game changer*.

My turned-around fear became 'They're afraid I'll reject them.'

And honestly? In most social situations, that's EXACTLY what happens.

I use this technique before every public speaking gig I do. I use it before I go into any new social situations where I fear I'll be judged and rejected too.

Know that you can turn it around.

Another trick is to ask myself, 'What's the worst that can happen?'

Really dare to go there.

I mean very-worst-case-scenario kind of going there.

Lots of light workers don't dare do this work, because they believe that we should only think positive thoughts in order to attract more positivity.

This witch? She disagrees.

If you've already imagined the worse-case scenario, you've already faced the very worst that can happen. You've seen it and felt it, which means you can then survive it and thrive.

Words have power

When we summon a deity by name, it is THAT deity who responds, not another.

Naming something gives power over that which is named.

When we name our fears, we can begin to witness and overcome them.

Be kind (but take no shit)

Be kind to yourself and others. If you spend valuable energy judging yourself and forcing yourself to spend time with people who demean you and make you feel bad about yourself, you'll strip yourself of your power.

And remember: a witch, first and foremost, is a woman in her power.

The truly powerful people in the world are kind, but they're not self-sacrificing. They see what's beautiful and wondrous, both within themselves and within others.

You can't be supportive of others if you're not supportive of yourself.

Important

Being kind doesn't mean becoming a complete pushover. You can be kind and have very clear boundaries about what is and isn't acceptable to you. I totally recommend practising that.

I do. Daily.

Be powerful and kind.

Notice what's around you (and a note on cultural appropriation)

Every culture has its own folklore, magic and mystical practices. If you're not sure of yours, talk to your family, trace your family heritage and ask questions of your aunties and grandmummas.

If they're no longer alive, ask them questions in dreamtime. Before you go to bed, either write a question in your journal asking them specifically to answer it, or ask it out loud naming the family member you'd like to answer it for you.

That's what I do anyway!

However you do it, get familiar with YOUR ancestral and cultural traditions. I always suggest starting 'at home' before diving head-first into the practices of another tradition, no matter how tantalizing and exciting Shamanism/Stregheria/Asatru might seem.

Important

If you find yourself drawn to a particular tradition, deity or spiritual path, I'm not saying you *shouldn't* follow the breadcrumbs.

Sometimes we just don't click with the lore of the land we live in. For example, I live in the UK, yet I'm from a Traveller tradition that means very little of the Celtic/British witchcraft traditions resonate with me. Instead, I have a strong call to the ancient Maltese goddesses, and to Kali Ma, Mary Magdalene and the Mayan Grandmothers and their female medicine magic.

If you feel called to a particular place or tradition, or to a particular goddess, it might be because you lived that tradition in another life. If you're called to a piece of jewellery with the Eye of Horus on it, it could be a sign that you need to look into Egyptian culture and its deities.

My advice? Be super-respectful, educate yourself, ask questions and deeply honour those who are indigenous to any particular tradition or practices you explore.

Be respectful and follow the breadcrumbs.

Experiment

Spend time under the moon, and touch and hold crystals to learn their properties. Talk to flowers, make runes, collect seashells, walk barefoot on the Earth and buy a tarot deck.

Witchcraft takes us back to the most natural, vibrant and raw parts of our soul; so find what feels good to you and then move towards it.

If you try something and it doesn't feel right, try something else. What works for one person may not for another. Change it up: there's no right or wrong way to do ANY of this.

Make your own way.

Expand your awareness

Go into nature and really feel how a tree feels. Feel its roots growing deep into the ground, and its branches reaching high to the sky. As you do that, step into what it is to be the tree.

Do this for a bird too. And for the ocean. And for a raincloud.

I'm fully aware of how crazy this might sound if communing with nature is new to you, but try it anyway.

I dare you.

Feel what it's like to no longer be separate.

Remember that you're a reflection of Mumma Nature. You, me and SHE are a force, a power source – we're not separate.

Know that you know

Know that all you need is already within you.

When you're truly a witch, you don't need to go to others for the answers. You don't even need this book.

It's simply a guide, a reminder of what you already know. The words, rituals and ceremonies I share are all just prompts to help you rediscover your power.

But you already knew that, right? Wink.

Being a witch
isn't what you do,
it's who you are.

Chapter 3

My Story

*Gypsies, Sara La Kali
and the Re-initiation*

*'The first time I called myself a "Witch" was
the most magical moment of my life.'*

— Margot Adler

To say I am a Gypsy is not *really* the truth.

Yes, I'm from Gypsy lineage, but I've never actually lived in a caravan or travelled with my home. My nanna did though: she travelled over from Ireland to settle on the south coast of the UK, which is where I was born.

Now I, like most people, love the romantic notion of Gypsies travelling in painted wagons, wearing big hoop earrings and reading tarot.

But the reality? Well, it's a little bit different.

Being of Gypsy descent meant I got called 'pikey' a lot.

It meant that I didn't fit in, and that I was made to feel fiercely unwelcome – both in the school playground and in social circles – on a daily basis.

Girls don't really go to school after thirteen in the Gypsy tradition, but I was obsessed with reading. In fact, my form of rebellion was to go full-out geek, and go on to university.

Back then, my nanna was a combination of the kitchen witch and the shuvihani I described earlier. People would come around to her house to ask for remedies and tinctures. They'd also ask for her insight, and she'd read their tea leaves.

Basically, she was the oracle of our 'hood. Respected and revered by everyone.

Gypsies are famous for their psychic powers and their ability to curse or bring good luck to those who cross their path. Some say that these powers are innate, passed down through a bloodline of countless generations of psychics and healers. And while I'd definitely agree, the very nature of Gypsy life means these powers can develop naturally too.

When I was really young, my mumma taught me how to observe the night sky, the working of the Earth and Mumma Nature. She taught me to look at the world through shamana eyes. (She totally did NOT call them that though.)

We'd watch cloud formations by day, and name star constellations by night. I didn't know it at the time, but she was teaching me witchcraft 101.

My nanna also taught me that everything was a 'sign' – bringing messages and/or warnings. My favourite? A single magpie is bad luck. Two, however? Well that represents joy. (As I'm typing, I've just looked out of my office window and two magpies are sitting on the lamp post. Seriously.)

I know that my body's cyclic nature is a direct reflection of Mumma Nature and her seasons of death and rebirth, because I witness and experience it in my very being.

I know that curses and blessings work and are real, because I've seen them both given and received.

I know that fortune telling and divination works, because I've seen my own visions become a reality. Over and over.

I see, feel and hear the presence of spirit.

These things are part of my daily life.

But – like my mumma – for a while there, I turned my back on the path – my heritage – along with the magic and the foresight that went with it.

Why?

Well, I became a teenager and I wanted to fit in. I was *tired* of being the pikey kid. I wanted to listen to pop music and kiss boys.

My mumma, relieved that I was no longer obsessed with learning everything my nanna knew, moved me to a new school and encouraged me to go against our tradition and get an education.

Then, in pursuit of total normality, she left my dad and me, and she married someone who could give her the thoroughly middle-class lifestyle she craved.

I barely saw her through my teen years, but my nanna and dad both supported my geekiness. So I went on to become a journalist, interviewing boybands for teen magazines, and working on Saturday morning TV.

I loved it, I was good at my job, the hours were crazy and the lifestyle was fast and fun.

Except, I wasn't connected to my body. I wasn't connected to nature. I wasn't connected to *anything*, not really.

I drank alcohol, barely slept, binge-ate in secret and loathed the body I was in. I always tried really hard to *achieve* the next goal and *do* the thing that would make people like me or give me praise.

But by turning my back on my lineage, I also turned my back on my magic, and my inherent, Goddess-given powers as a woman.

And the Goddess, the divine feminine – who I now call SHE – sent out a distress flare in the form of endometriosis and polycystic ovary syndrome.

She created pain and dis-ease in my womb space so painful that I was forced to reassess EVERYTHING.

I couldn't do my work any more because I was in so much pain, and I was bleeding more days than I wasn't each month.

It was all so bloody inconvenient. **Pun totally intended.**

What I know now is that the pain was occurring to call me home. Home to myself, to my body, to my magic and my roots.

Literally and figuratively.

You can read about that in much more detail in my book *Love Your Lady Landscape*; but ultimately, I began a journey of reconnection, remembrance and reverence for SHE.

For Her.

It was a reclamation of my womb, my roots, my power and my magic.

At exactly the same time that my nanna left her body.

The way of the witch means there are *no* coincidences.

After that, my nan, who'd died some years previously, spoke to me in my dreamtime often. She showed me images of the herbs and teas we used to make together. She gave me ingredient lists of herbs that would make teas to ease my period pain, tinctures to reduce inflammation and balms to soothe cramps.

These dreamtime downloads led me not only to explore my own Gypsy roots, but to get curious about what it really meant to *me* to be a witch.

My nan and mumma both left notebooks, which some witches called Grimoires, with recipes, dreams and spells, many of which I'm still deciphering.

I got geeky about local witches and covens on the south coast of the UK. I recommend reading *every* book by Sybil Leek and Doreen Valiente: two super-influential south-coast witches. I'm also blessed that I've been able to learn and practise magic with sisters who work with Mayan medicine and Italian Strega.

However, I still always come back to my roots, because the Gypsy tradition uses simple spells and rituals to harness the power of nature and the elemental spirits all around us.

Gypsies don't believe that you need an intermediary between you and God/Goddess/Spirit/All That Is or the 'Powers that be' as my nannas called it.

Nor do I.

I keep everything as simple as I can, personally.
I think that's how magic should be.

Remember your magic.

Remember you're magic.

Meet Sara La Kali

Sara La Kali is the patron saint of the Gypsies.

My nanna had a picture of her in a frame in the hallway. And she's my patron too, in that when I whisper/scream/shout/cry/sweat my prayers, they're usually to her.

Some believe that Sara La Kali – Black Sara – was the daughter of Jesus and Mary Magdalene.

Another claim is that she was the servant of the Marys (Mary Magdalene, Marie-Salome and Marie-Jacobe), who arrived with them on the shores of Southern France from Palestine after the resurrection of Christ. However, there's no mention of her in the Gospels or in the early descriptions of the pilgrimage.

Another version is that she was a Gypsy woman who was schooled in the esoteric wisdom of her people, who was living in the Camargue when she welcomed Mary ashore.

There are no relics for Sara La Kali.

She's not even an official saint of the Catholic Church, but her effigy is found in the local church in Saintes-Maries-de-la-Mer, and the Gypsies love her. Every year, on her feast day, 25 May, Gypsies travel from all over the world to pay homage to her.

Her statue is kept underground, in the church's crypt: an unimposing doll-like, dark-skinned figure. She's dressed in several colourful robes made by Gypsy women, which are presented to her each and every year.

During her festival, those who seek her healing and blessings come to touch her skirts. They put scarves around her neck, offer flowers, light candles and give thanks for the miracles and prayers answered in the preceding years. They pay her homage in the Gypsy Prayer, a copy of which sits framed at her feet.

It's through her that Mary Magdalene
and the Black Madonna are related.

Even the crown that sits upon her head holds a symbolic key. In it rest thirteen pearls, recalling the lunar cycle, and the pearl that is both Aphrodite's and Mary's sacred jewel.

The crown twinkles in the light from the hundreds of candles lit in her honour, which throw out an amazing amount of heat.

Men and women form a reverential queue in order to have a few moments with her. They touch her robes, they kiss her, they leave photos of their departed loved ones and they pin notes and trinkets to her clothing.

Meeting her is an intense, emotional encounter.

Elders on white horses take her statue from near the church and carry it in a procession, through narrow streets strewn with roses, to the sea. Gypsies in their traditional dress immerse the statue in the ocean, taking all the problems that petitioners brought her out to sea.

Everyone enters the water, where they too can be washed of their problems. It's an act of purification to be washed by the sea after this ritual.

It's really not dissimilar to how Hindus traditionally worship their gods and goddesses in India: immersing them in the Ganges river after performing puja rites on the major holy days. (Except in Saintes-Maries-de-la-Mer, they rescue her from the water and place her back in the basement.)

Some say Sara La Kali is a form of Kali, the Hindu goddess of death. My homegirl.

Kali means 'black' in both Sanskrit and Romani, the language still spoken by many European Gypsies.

I like to think that, for the purpose of appeasing the Catholic Church, Kali was hidden inside another story. The story of the sacred and divine feminine is that of Sara.

The Gypsies couldn't very well tell the clergy, 'By the way, we're keeping our goddess of death and destruction in your basement!' now, could they? It's in the darkness that roots grow deepest;

and in that basement, the divine feminine has continued to grow strong.

The story I've been told is that Sara La Kali came from noble lineage. (Some even say that she IS the holy grail, but that? Well, that's a whole other book and story.) She knew and taught the secrets, rites and mysteries of the Isis temple, like those taught by Mary Magdalene herself.

To me, she's the daughter of MM and Jesus; and she's one of the many manifestations of what we call the Mother Goddess, the goddess of creation. Whether earlier Dark Mothers were called Kali, Cybele, Isis or any other name, it doesn't make much difference.

To us, Sara La Kali is the mother of the Gypsies.

My husband (the Viking) and I got handfasted on 25 May in homage to her; and we were sprinkled with sea water from Saintes-Maries-de-la-Mer.

Sara La Kali is known for her powers to heal. She also offers guidance in business and can help to cleanse your past (bad habits, bad boys, bad luck – that kind of thing). If you feel you're being blocked, have enemies or someone is out to get you, Sara La Kali is your girl.

You can also call on her for good luck, fertility, healing and general success in business matters.

Basically, she's a badass.

◌ How to Pay Homage ◌ to Sara La Kali

What you'll need:

- A red candle
- Rose absolute oil

What to do:

You can pay homage or petition Sara La Kali by anointing a red candle with rose oil, and lighting it. Then, for three nights when the moon is full, repeat the following petition three times:

'Sara, patron saint of Travellers and Gypsies the world over, I'd love to find you here.

To tell you all that I have in my heart, and in you confide my sorrows and my joys.

Sara, please come to me now.'

Then either write, say out loud, or whisper your prayers to Sara La Kali. Ask her for guidance.

FYI: She's also really supportive to those who've lost their way. Which is pretty much all of us at one time or another, right?

⌒◌⌒

The Re-initiation

I mentioned earlier that I don't think you need to be initiated to become a witch, and this is definitely still true. But in 2008, after turning my back on my lineage and exploring new witch-led paths, I wanted more than anything to be re-initiated in the way of the witch.

I wanted to take back what was mine: my power and authority as a woman. So instead of turning to a coven with a high priestess to initiate and validate me, I initiated myself.

I initiated myself by doing the very thing that the persecutors of witches had previously used to torture and kill them.

I immersed myself naked in a sacred spring.

Not just any spring, but the White Spring in Glastonbury.

The White Spring is found in the womb of Glastonbury Tor: a beautiful hill with St Michael's tower sitting proudly on top, overlooking what many believe to be Avalon.

I'd spent the three years previous to my initiation travelling back and forth to Glastonbury. It's a small English market town, world-renowned for being a place of pilgrimage for spiritual seekers; and for being steeped in mysticism and spiritual folklore.

I had friends who lived there who invited me to stay with them to rest and heal and mend my broken womb and heart. (John and Cheryl, I will forever be grateful to you for the sanctuary you provided for me in those years.)

Glastonbury has many witchcraft, spiritual and new age shops in its high street. But that's not where you'll find the magic.

Instead, the magic is in her landscape.

And for me, the White Spring is the centre of that magic.

People would gather in the womb of the Tor at Sabbats and the turn of the seasons to sing, drum and chant. The well keepers at the time, Max and Lisa, are the very best of bards and storytellers; and they'd share stories, poems and songs dedicated to the gods and goddesses of the season and the land.

So on a July morning, I decided that I'd initiate myself by way of immersion. And I'd do it in defiance of all the persecutors who'd dunked those they accused of being witches. (If you drowned, they knew you weren't a witch. Except… you were dead.)

The White Spring, which is essentially a dark, candle-lit, cave-like dwelling – a well house – held so much magic and memory for me. In its northwest corner, there's a seven-foot plunge well – I know how deep it is now, but I didn't then. The well is round, with a stone wall, like a ledge, surrounding it. And it's overlooked by a beautiful black Madonna.

My friend John, one of the local guardians of the well (the guardians are support for the well keepers, so that the well is always tended to), gave me exclusive access. We lit candles together and he closed the door, leaving me in the womb of the Tor alone.

I took off my clothes, leaving only an obsidian necklace that I'd been called to buy earlier that day to represent my initiation. It was a talisman – a token to imbue with the magic of what was happening – around my neck.

I tentatively climbed up to the ledge of the well, where I looked into the eyes of the black Madonna, who for me represents the Dark

Mother. Then I whispered my prayer to her: the hymn to the Divine Mother as shared by China Galland in her book *Longing for Darkness*:

Alas, I do not know either the mystical word or the mystical diagram, nor do I know the song of praise to thee, nor how to welcome thee, nor how to meditate on thee. Nor how to inform thee of my distress.

But this much I know o' mother, that to take refuge in thee is to destroy all miseries.

(It's NO coincidence that I was re-reading this book the day my mumma left her body. And when I woke up, sobbing in the night after her death, I picked up the book for comfort, and it opened to this prayer.)

I sat on the edge of the well.

I felt my own edges.

I was in a dark cave, in front of the Dark Mother, about to immerse myself in the darkness.

The darkness, where Patriarchy had put my power and the power all of the women in my family who'd gone before.

'I'm not scared of the dark,' I told myself out loud. I told Her. I told SHE.

I was ready to claim that power back.

I slid off the edge, not knowing how deep the well actually was, and I immersed myself. Fully.

Cellular memory released as soon as I was underwater.

I heard screams and wails. I remembered times when my tongue had been cut from my mouth for speaking my truth; and as I re-emerged, because I AM a witch after all, I looked at the black Madonna and she whispered, 'It's safe for you to be powerful.'

It IS safe for me to be powerful.

It IS safe for me to be in my power.

It is safe for YOU to be powerful.

It is safe for YOU to be in your power.

Since then, I've initiated myself in the way of the witch over and over again.

Some initiations I've chosen: I've walked on fire, I've worked with shamans and plant teachers, as well as the frog medicine, Kambo.

I've been initiated by Mayan grandmothers into the ways of the wise womb. I celebrated my menarche in ritual and ceremony at the age of 32; and I was given access to the Mnajdra and Hagar Qim temples in Malta to call back my power.

There were other initiations too, like the death of both my parents in the space of a month. In fact, my entire family died in that eighteen-month period: mum, dad, two uncles, three aunties and a cousin who was the same age as me.

I had to negotiate the world from THAT place: the loss, the pain, and being plunged into the depths of perpetual darkness, thinking I'd never return. More importantly, I didn't *want* to return, having felt like I'd been thrown into the flames, submerged underwater AND been buried alive all at the same time.

But guess what?

> **I didn't burn. I didn't drown. I didn't suffocate.**
> **I DID die though.**
> **I died to who and what I no longer was. But with EVERY initiation, I was also reborn a little bit more powerful than the time before.**

It's safe for me
to be powerful.

Chapter 4

Her Story

The Great Mumma,
Patriarchy and
the Witch Hunts

Why do we have to remember that we are powerful?

Why have we forgotten?

Why do we remember, then forget all over again?

Why do we have to wake and reclaim the witch now more than ever before?

Patriarchy.

Note: When I talk about Patriarchy, I'm not man bashing. I'm not bashing Christianity either. When you read what I'm about to tell you, you'll realize we've ALL been played by Patriarchy: men AND women.

What I share is a response, my personal response, to the half-truths and no-truths we've been told about women, witches and the witch hunts.

This can't be intellectualized. It needs to be felt.

Fully.

In your body.

Y'see, the simple act of looking at, studying and exploring what happened in history (His Story) changes it.

The facts may have been written down at the time, but what was the agenda of the man who wrote them?

Remember: women were rarely allowed to write until the nineteenth century. At that point, the birth of the suffragette movement meant that women began to demand a place alongside men in the world. They demanded to contribute to cultural discourse, to make their opinions heard and to tell their own stories. (High fives and deep bows to them for that.)

But before that? Well, *His Story* was, and still is in most cases, written by the victor. And who was the victor in the witch hunts?

It certainly wasn't the women.

So even the story we've been told about the witch hunts was written by men. Men whose agenda it was to maintain the Church's supremacy, and to suppress and repress connection, community and shared wisdom.

So when each of us looks at any moment in His Story, when we get inquisitive about it and then share our version of it, we create a new version of it. And the version we create changes it, depending on our thoughts, feelings and beliefs.

Even now, with so many of us awake to how we're continually played and manipulated by the media, it's still very hard to get the actual truth about things.

TV companies have sponsors and owners who want things told their way. Countries and governments want (and need) us to believe and behave in a certain way. Every story that's told has a spin or colour placed on it by those who share it.

Me included.

I'll be totally upfront and honest with you right now. My agenda in writing this book and telling you everything in it is simple: I want you to take back what's rightfully yours as a woman.

ALL OF IT.

**The challenge – specifically for women,
whose story has been censored, silenced,
repressed and burned over the last
3,000 years – is to question EVERYTHING.**

I invite you to feel into the truth behind the actions you hear or read about. Get curious. What was the motivation?

Then really listen for the echoes of truth that have been passed down through the generations of ancestral trauma and karma that you carry in each and every cell.

Find the truth that echoes inside YOU.

What's the Story?

For centuries now, we've been living in a society that has no respect or love for womankind. But it wasn't always like that.

The term *witch* was once used interchangeably with *wise woman* or *healer*. It was used to describe a wise woman who'd completed her bleeding years – the years where she'd gathered her wisdom with each and every menstrual cycle. And having completed those years, she'd arrived in the seat of her power, from which she'd teach ancestral knowledge.

The word *hag* once referred to women who refused to conform or bow down to patriarchal expectations. Hags were wilful and badass.

Now, though, despite having such seemingly empowering qualities, hags and witches have been reframed to represent the *undesirable*.

Why undesirable? Because independence, wilfulness and badass-ery are *not* qualities that men have historically found attractive in women. And that's precisely what defines a patriarchal society: one in which men make the rules and women are simply 'unassuming' and 'passive' participants.

But like I said above: it hasn't always been this way.

The Great Mumma

Before *His* story, there was *Her* story.

A time when a woman's stomach mysteriously swelling, and then nine moons later producing a baby from between her legs, was one of *the* most awe-inspiring acts of lady magic ever witnessed.

That she could also produce food – life-sustaining milk from her breasts – made it pretty evident that she was a direct reflection of the nurturing and providing elements of Mumma Nature.

The oldest work of prehistoric art ever discovered, the Venus of Willendorf, is a small clay statue of a fertile woman. She has an abundant stomach, twerk-worthy bum and huge pendulous breasts.

She's a representation of the fertility goddess worshipped in those times; and she's evolved into the multifaceted Goddess that many witches love and worship today. The same Goddess I call SHE.

Malta, a small cluster of islands in the Mediterranean sea, was an epicentre for SHE. Full-bodied, 10-foot-tall statues of bountiful, abundant women representing Mother Earth proudly stood outside the temples there.

Ancient societies had priestesses: the women of the temples of Artemis and Diana in ancient Greece and Rome, the Oracle of Apollo at Delphi and the Celtic priestesses of Britain.

All these wise ones were keepers of arcane, sacred knowledge. They had many skills, including the sacred observation of seasonal customs, healing, star craft, divination, seeing the future, and understanding and recognizing the roots of that future in the past and present.

They also held sacred the spiritual lives of the communities they served.

This knowledge was stored and kept safe, with most of it being passed down orally through words and song, committed to memory rather than books. And for the most part, as you'd hope in any spiritual organization or temple, it was shared without competition or fear, and with great love and respect.

For thousands of years, people from all over the world worshipped a mother god: the Great Mother. She was nature and nurture, death and rebirth, fierce and loving, light and dark. She was the polarities and all the mystery that lies in between them. This creatrix of all that is was known as both male and female; and a divine, sacred and devotional relationship with her was our guide.

So it's no coincidence that when we were intentionally disconnected from the Great Mumma – when our goddess nature was banished from the Roman Catholic church – both men and women became disconnected from who they were.

The Patriarchal Takeover

We were bereft of a parent.

Our mumma.

The one who nourished us.

Enter Patriarchy, predominantly Christianity, to take on the role of parent.

A controlling, ego-fuelled, money-obsessed, capitalist parent.

The idea that we experienced our body as sacred, that we lived in community and that we worked for love and service was not conducive to the development of capitalism.

So what followed was the destruction of ALL of that: community, connection and the sharing of wisdom were replaced by greed, control and ego.

The Church, wealthy landowners and merchant classes wanted to turn the lower classes into a work machine – a workforce that'd be compliant and work for money. The only way they could do that was to turn the mystical into a machine.

They needed to steal and repress our spiritual beliefs, take away any sacred practices of initiation into adulthood, and disconnect us from any 'magical' concept that meant we had agency and power.

Without a mumma, both men and women remain infantilized. They're filled with fear daily to maintain obedience and amenability. That makes them unable to take responsibility for themselves.

And Patriarchy has continued to create firm structures to keep us that way right through to the times we're currently living in.

Let's pause and think about THAT for a moment.

For women, these patriarchal constructs are far-reaching, and the list is never-ending. Some examples of how they look today (because yes, we've come a long way, but ohmygoddess, there's still a LONG way to go) include mansplaining, the gender pay gap, revenge porn, porn in general, hair removal, violence… Insert your own way that Patriarchy wants you to think you're broken and need fixing here.

This patriarchal takeover was not instant.

Despite Christianity becoming the established religion all over Europe, Pagans still originally totally outnumbered Christians. So the Church made Pagan gods and goddesses recognizable as Christian saints, and Pagan feast days remained Christian holidays.

For example, 25 December – four days after the Winter Solstice – was chosen to bring Pagan sun worshippers into the Christian church. Since this was originally their feast day, it was far easier to change the name of the holiday and its symbolism than it was to invent a brand new holiday on another day.

But when Christians did finally establish themselves, they were ready to begin their persecution and eradication of all things Pagan.

It was at this point that Paganism went underground, and its religious and spiritual practices started being called 'evil'.

Suddenly, the Great Mother was made to serve as Christ's virgin mother – her sexuality erased, deleted and no longer necessary. Her power was reduced from that of Mother Nature, creatrix of the entire freakin' world, to a sterile intermediary between man and a male god.

While I was writing this book, on a Goddess-led trip to Glastonbury with my friend, actress and creatrix Carrie Anne Moss, we visited Halo Avalon: a shop at the top of the high street. In there, we found a dirty, chalk-white statue of Mary without hands.

When I held the statue, she told me: 'Do you know why I've got no hands? Because I'm done with carrying this bullshit story of being clean and sanitized. Yes, I was a virgin; but only in its truest sense: a woman unto herself. So if we're taking back the word "witch", can we please take back the word "virgin" too?'

Obviously, I bought her; and she's currently sitting on my desk as I write.

FYI

Ishtar, Diana, Astarte and Isis were all called Virgin too, but that didn't mean 'sexually chaste' as Christianity has had us believe. Instead, it meant 'sexually independent'. A woman unto herself.

Basically, badass.

Monica Sjoo and Barbara Mor outline in their book *The Great Cosmic Mother: Rediscovering the Religion of the Earth* that virgins were literally 'free women'. They were women who were 'one in themselves', i.e. not yet legally owned by their husbands.

In fact, the very word 'virgin' derives from a Latin root meaning strength, force and skill.

So, note to Mary: Mary, you're my homegirl; and Lady, we're taking it back.

ALL OF IT.

What Happened Next

Stamping out religions and relentlessly disconnecting us from our power was carried out in many, many ways. Changing the terminology of words like 'virgin' to take away any kind of powerful connotation? Well, that was simply one of them.

Other ways were terrifying and cruel, and they've meant that society (and women, specifically) still carry the bone-deep echo of fear, shame and confusion within themselves.

The 'Witch' Hunts

Before Christianity pushed the worship of the Great Mumma underground, our unique relationship to the process of reproduction – our menstrual blood and cyclic nature – was revered. Giving birth was seen as participating in a magical miracle.

That meant women were credited with a special understanding of the secrets of nature – secrets that enabled them to influence life and death, understand sexuality and discover the hidden properties of things.

Practising magic (and when I say 'magic', I mean the practical, everyday magic that women created as healers, herbalists, midwives and potion-makers – not spells or glamour tricks) was a source of power for many women. This is why, I believe, women became the primary targets as Patriarchy set to work converting the mystical into a machine.

NOTE: Witch hunts happened predominantly to women – but there were 'unsuitable' men who perished too. Gay men, vagrants, male Gypsies, Jews and foreigners/'strangers' were all persecuted – albeit in far fewer numbers than women.

Patriarchy couldn't control a woman's 'magic' or her ability to create 'weakness' in the otherwise-compliant work machine by enticing and manipulating men through her sexuality and female power.

And that meant that Patriarchy needed to demonize women and their 'powers'.

It started in 1484 with Pope Innocent VIII. Based on the Bible statement 'Thou shalt not suffer a witch to live' (Exodus 22:18), which outlines and describes the 'supposed' activities of witches, he gave the Church authority to find witches and kill them, denying them all rights to a fair trial.

And a 'witch', for the Church, was any strong woman.

Women who were healers (and midwives in particular) were labelled witches and killed, because the men who were graduating from universities and becoming doctors at the time wanted to control the medical world. They wanted *absolute* authority – authority that couldn't be questioned by the women who were, in most cases, much more experienced, yet had no official standing.

To those doctors, women were a major threat.

It was a healer holocaust.

Witchcraft was defined as a 'crimen exceptum': an exceptional crime, distinct from all others. Ordinary punishments would simply not be enough.

The patriarchal institution wanted to break down and *destroy* the strong, powerful women who threatened them. They wanted women to fear them – and each other – so that they never knew, or experienced, the magic and power that they had within them.

They wanted to dismember the Goddess and the divine spark of sisterhood in women that she represented.

The accusations became ridiculous.

If you had a cat...

If you spoke to animals...

If you were skilled in herb lore...

If your neighbour disliked you...

If you knew the secret meanings of numbers, cards, stones and the future...

If you knew how to birth a baby, ease a woman through childbirth or prevent conception...

The fact that sexuality was stifled and seen as evil created a ripe environment in which women could be harmed, tortured and killed.

The Hammer of the Witches

In 1486, Heinrich Kramer wrote the book *Malleus Maleficarum*, which translates roughly to 'Hammer of the Witches'. It is quite possibly the most misogynistic text EVER written, and it became the how-to guide for 'catching a witch' throughout Europe.

Don't read it: it'll make you angry. In fact, DO read it and get really bloody angry.

It was initially written to justify, support and enforce the Pope's Papal Bull. It acknowledged the existence of demons (but inverted their true nature: daemons are animal spirits who guide us, and sometimes teach us sharp, harsh lessons) and devils. It also talked about evil spirits that haunted, taunted and cursed the population.

It claimed that witches made pacts with these demons to help with crops and birth, with curing ailments, preventing conception and killing their enemies.

Other versions of this story say that it was 'witches' themselves who created the plague.

Either way, thanks to this text, 'witches' – and by that I mean women – were rarely going to get out alive.

Dangerous Women

'Never in history have women been subjected to such
a massive, internationally organized, legally approved,
religiously blessed assault on their bodies.'
— SILVIA FEDERICI

Hundreds of thousands of women were arrested, stripped naked and completely shaved – often in the presence of men.

They were pricked with long needles in every part of their bodies in search of the 'devil mark'. These needles were often concealed in seemingly blunt silver rods that were said to be able to detect a witch.

The examiner would run the rod over a woman's naked body; then, undetected, push a button to make the needle pierce her at random points. Of course, that would make her scream, proving herself to be a witch because she couldn't handle a seemingly blunt silver rod touching her.

And this was by no means the end of their torments. The most sadistic tortures ever invented were inflicted on the bodies of accused women, which provided an ideal laboratory for the development of pain and torture.

Federici believes: 'The most sadistic tortures ever invented were inflicted on the bodies of accused women, which provided an ideal laboratory for the development of pain and torture.'

The truth that women became stronger in belonging was broken. Persecutors encouraged sisters to turn on each other in order to save themselves, and entire matrilineal chains were torn apart.

Older women were persecuted too, as they were the ones who remembered. They went from home to home, circulating stories, sharing secrets and wisdom and weaving together past and present events.

In doing so, they became a threat to the modernizers, who were determined to destroy the past and undo customs and relationships.

In her book *Caliban and the Witch* (PLEASE READ THIS BOOK: it's heavy going, but it's so worth it!) Silvia Federici says that the witch hunts introduced a system of terror to ALL women. And from that system emerged a new, much more acceptable model of femininity to which women would have to conform in order to be socially accepted in the developing capitalist society.

That model was one in which:

- Women were sexless, obedient and submissive.

- Women's bodies and their life-giving menstrual blood were now receptacles of shame and sin.

- Women were resigned to being subordinate to men.

- Women accepted their role as reproducers of life, and accepted too that in a capitalist society, that role was devalued to being simply 'their job'.

Women too became a machine.

Right up until this very day, historians have tended to wipe out the witch trials. They fail to mention that over 13 million women were killed on nooses, on torture racks and with flames. There were many, many ways in which the erasure of women become totally acceptable in Renaissance Europe and North America.

Such a deletion from history is consistent with the initial goals of the witch trials. The history of witches is, after all, a history of the persecution of women – or as author and theorist Erica Jong called it, a 'gendercide.'

The more we fear the witch, the more we fear our own power – which was, and still is, exactly the point of patriarchal propaganda.

Telling my version of the 'witch' hunts, and by that I mean femicide – even in its bare-boned state as I've done here – *will* awaken many memories within us.

In fact, I've tried to sit down to write this chapter so many times. EVERY time I've been hit with a need-to-go-lie-in-a-dark-room migraine. Or a sore neck. Or a need to be violently sick.

This is NOT a coincidence.

Remember

Feel into those echoes of truth that have been passed down through the generations of ancestral trauma and karma and find the truth that echoes inside of YOU.

We can't change His
Story, but we do get
to rewrite Her Story.

OUR Story.

Chapter 5

Our Story

Reclaiming the Witch,
Reclaiming Your Power

Fast-forward to a conflicted and confused 21st century, where we're told as women that we've smashed so many of the restrictions of Patriarchy, and yet:

- Eating disorders continue to rise.

- Cosmetic surgery is the fastest-growing medical procedure.

- Sales of female beauty products have tripled.

- Pornography is one of the most widely consumed forms of media.

Our freedom as women is superficial.

Sure, on the surface, it *seems* that we can work and vote. But that 'freedom' is infused with self-hatred, physical obsessions, terror of aging and mistrust of other women.

Older women fear younger ones; and young women fear old.

And it's all a direct result of the shame and humiliation inflicted by the torture and torment of the witch trials.

Does this ring a bell?

It should.

Just like the patriarchs who initiated the witch hunts, today's patriarchs benefit from keeping us oppressed and perpetually mistrusting each other.

Yep, making mothers and daughters testify against each other during the witch trials (and declaring it was all in the name of the Mother Church) has created a womb-deep mistrust amongst women. And it's one that totally messes up friendships, mother-and-daughter relationships and sisterhood today.

Male-dominated institutions are threatened by women's freedom, so they exploit female guilt and foster apprehension about our bodies.

But...

... What would the pornography industry do if women refused to re-enact male desires?

... What would the cosmetic surgery industry do if women embraced the unchanging beauty within them, instead of obsessing about the ever-changing patriarchal representations of external beauty?

... What would the beauty and self-help/diet industries do if women trusted that all the knowledge and wisdom they ever needed was already inside them (and that it could be accessed by connecting with the power of their menstrual cycles)?

These questions aren't meant to put even more pressure and responsibility on you as a woman. I just want to highlight that there are *billions* of pounds invested in keeping you subordinate and not loving your sweet self.

In other words: misogyny and sexism make money.

Generations of women have been disconnected from the power that lies between their thighs – their lady landscape, their womb and their menstrual cycle. They've lost connection with their ability to create life (and everything else) in their wombs, which means their minds can be easily manipulated and indoctrinated by Patriarchy.

And this, in turn, means that both men *and* women now heavily rely on women remaining small and contained.

Are you angry and rage-full yet?

I'd understand if you weren't. Like me, you've probably also been taught that it's not okay to be angry. Or at least that it's not okay to show it.

It's like a cell-deep written memo from Patriarchy stating that 'emoting' and 'feeling' are NOT an option. If you do either, you know that you'll be shamed for it. You'll be deemed 'too much', 'hormonal' and in some cases, 'dangerous'. (These are all good things, BTW. They just don't want *you* to know that.)

It's all part of the indoctrination.

The Fear, the Witch and the Wound

We live in a cultural climate that makes women feel perpetually guilty for simply being women.

This is the modern-day equivalent of the Inquisition. Only, instead of terrorizing us with accusations, torture and public executions, Patriarchy has made us torture ourselves.

We put ourselves on trial every time we look in the mirror – and before the trial begins, we already know that we're guilty.

In fact, while I was writing this book, I actually rang my editor and told her: 'I don't want to write the Witch book any more.'

I said, 'I'll pay back my advance. I don't want to do it.'

Why?

Well, I was on Day 28 of my menstrual cycle (my inner critic works overtime in my premenstrual phase), the moon was full and powerful and I felt the *fear*.

Fear is the most powerful torture of all.

Fear festers deep in the feminine wound, so all Patriarchy has to do is kick back and let us turn our own screws/light our own matches/cut our own ropes.

My editor, Amy – who is an agent of SHE and a soul sister, as well as someone who works her magic with words – talked me through it.

Through the fear, the wounding and the judgement.

And this isn't the first time she's had to do it. (I'm guessing it won't be the last either.)

She reminded me of a similar conversation we had when my last book *Love Your Lady Landscape* was just about to go for its final edit.

I'd felt the fear of being seen, heard, judged and punished for my beliefs and actions then too.

And now, I felt it again.

When it comes to sharing stories – *these* stories, *our* stories – it feels like a real, gaping, bloody, vagina-like gash of a wound. This wound is personal, societal, generational and matrilineal.

This wound has many forms, and it's been passed down through our very cells.

It's in our ancestral memory.

It's a wound of many, many forms.

It's a wound of the women who've gone before me.

It's the wound of my mumma, who turned her back on her psychic and seer-like powers for fear of being called a witch.

It's the wound of my nanna, who'd never speak the word 'witch', yet that's exactly what she was. And the whole neighbourhood *knew* it.

It's a wound of past lives.

Yep, this is not my first rodeo sharing women's wisdom.

Doing women's work.

Being a witch.

In at least one lifetime, I had my tongue cut from my mouth in front of the women I was talking to.

In another, I was the victim of a witch hunt where other women that I believed to be kindred – sisters and friends – called me out to the authorities; and I was drowned.

It's a wound of THIS lifetime.

Even in this present life, I've been mishandled, smacked, shamed, judged and disrespected by both men AND women.

Yet, I KNOW I'm here to be an advocate for the women who may not have had their tongues sliced, but whose voices are still being silenced and censored. Who still aren't being heard.

I've said this MANY times, but do you think I'd be talking about periods and vaginas and witches and all things taboo if I actually had a choice?

Do you think I'd *choose* to keep putting myself out there, over and over again? Do you think I'd *choose* to write books that aren't easy to market – that talk about SHE and how our wombs are a power source? Do you think I'd *choose* to declare that I'm a witch, and wake other witches – creating yet more ways for others potentially to ridicule, judge and shame me?

But it *is* what I've signed up for.

I'm here to show that witch hunts are *still* happening.

As I write this book, my father-in-love is in Mexico for the Day of the Dead celebrations. He sent me a picture of an outside altar set up in memory of female homicide victims: women who've been killed *this* year by the Mexican government. Their crime? Being women.

The Western world version of modern-day witch hunts can be witnessed in any trash mag or reality TV show. In them, you'll see women being called out, judged and 'burned' by mainstream and social media. So know that the fear some of us feel about sharing our story, our truths and our vulnerabilities isn't made up, 'perceived' or merely historical.

It's real.

Which is why the fact you're reading this book, the fact you've heard The Call, is so bloody important.

Speak Your Truth (Even If Your Voice Shakes)

> Our deepest wounds, our fears, are what
> we need to teach and share the most.

That past life where my tongue had been cut from my mouth? It's one I've since visited many times in past life regressions; and it's explained so much of my experience around 'speaking' out loud and having a voice in this lifetime.

Y'see, since I was a kid, I've had a fear about speaking out loud.

I'm not just talking adrenalin-fuelled nerves here, but actual keep-me-awake-at-night-I'm-going-to-die-if-I-speak-out-loud fear.

And I also remember that for about five years when I was a kid, I had this one recurring dream. I was a woman, wearing red robes somewhere hot and dusty with whitewashed buildings.

I was talking to women who were looking at me, and I remember looking deep into their eyes as I spoke in another language. Suddenly, two big, burly men wearing dark blue robes that covered their faces pushed me to the floor, held me down and cut out my tongue.

I now know, thanks to the White Spring immersion that triggered the memory of that recurring dream, that the two are *not* unrelated.

Over the last few years, it's all started to make sense. For four years of my childhood I was mute, I literally didn't speak a word. Throughout school and university, I couldn't understand why I never raised my hand in class, or why I pretended to be sick to avoid doing a presentation. I even took a lower grade for my final university assessment rather than take the spoken exam.

I had throat infections that left me voiceless throughout my teenage years and into my late twenties.

Then, when my first ever book came out with a big swanky publisher, I did a lot of public speaking training. I thought I was ready, but the day I was due to do a national radio show, I lost my voice.

It all added up over time to a point where my fear of speaking out loud created a completely mute reality.

Now, you may not struggle the way I do to speak out loud. But I'm pretty certain that in some way, somehow, as a woman, you've experienced being silenced or shhh-ed. Maybe you've experienced 'mansplaining' – when a man explains something to a woman in a condescending, patronizing way.

Maybe you've been spoken over, called names, trolled or silenced (verbally, psychologically or physically); and you too have felt the fear.

And if you have?

You are NOT alone.

Every time I write a book or a blog post. Every time I stand on stage or begin an interview. I feel it.

For some women, that fear might be perceived and societal. For others it might be real and experiential: either from past lives or from this one.

But here's the deal.

Here's what I've had to learn every time I say yes to doing a podcast, a TV or radio interview or speaking on a big stage, when what I *really* wanted to do was say 'no' and stay in my PJs:

In order to share our powerful SHE medicine, our magic, our unique-to-us-flavour in the world, we have to be seen AND heard.

And for many of us (me included), that doesn't come easy.

The fear that it's 'not safe' for us to speak/write/share our story – which is our ultimate medicine to the world – can keep us mute.

And THAT renders our powers completely useless.

SHE demands that in reclaiming the witch, we reclaim our power.

You might not have to stand in front of people and speak out loud on radio and TV.

Still though, you're being asked to trust yourself and your voice. To trust your body and your knowing. To speak up for what you believe in, and to be a megaphone for those who are oppressed and who don't have a voice.

If you have a social media platform, you're being called to have an opinion. To potentially disagree with people you care about in order to share your truth and what's real for you.

I haven't got it figured out, BTW.

I shake, I stutter and I ummm and ahhh.

I don't speak in soundbites, but what I've come to realize is that *how* I show up is irrelevant. It's in the act of showing up itself that we *really* claim the power back.

So I keep showing up: imperfect and unedited. And not always by choice, if I'm honest. For the most part, I'd MUCH rather sit in a blanket fort, sipping tea, eating peanut butter and banana on toast and reading a good book.

I feel the fear *every time* I hit the record button on a video or step out onto a stage. The fear of being the accused woman, tied with iron clamps and given to the fire.

Yet I keep showing up, and I stand rooted in the unedited, sometimes messy and very rarely glossy experience of *my* truth.

I share from where I'm at, to give other women the permission to do the same.

This, for me, feels like how it used to be.

Y'know, before we forgot.

BP (Before Patriarchy).

Before our voices were stolen.

Back when women were oracles.

Back when the space between our thighs was considered a power portal with a direct hook-up to source. Back when our menstrual cycle was honoured and respected as a way to explore the light *and* the dark of who we are, and experience the seasons of Mumma Nature in a menstrual month.

When women were a source of knowledge.

When women were *the* source.

When we trusted ourselves.

When we trusted our wisdom.

When we trusted our power.

When we weren't trolled on social media, or made to feel small, inadequate or less-than for having voices and opinions.

When we didn't keep second-guessing ourselves, or worry what other people thought of us.

When we were unapologetic truth tellers.

What the world wants and needs – and damn it, what *I* want and need – is for us to share our stories, our medicine and our *real* (by which I mean our whole, raw, vulnerable messy glorious truths).

Earlier in the chapter, I listed just *some* of the gazillion ways in which our voices are stolen on a daily basis. And when I acknowledge them, it makes it hard for me to ask you to remember, repeat and take on the mantra that the black Madonna of the White Spring gave me during my initiation on that July morning:

'It is safe for me to be powerful.'

But I *am* asking you to take it on. And I'm asking you to repeat it over and over and over again. As women, it's our responsibility to make it safe for each other to be powerful.

It's time for us to tell OUR story. Because the story we tell is the world we make.

Real voices. Not the voice of the 'good girl' who says what she thinks others want her to say so they'll like her more. Not an over-rehearsed speech. Not a carbon-copy of someone else's truth.

Your truth.

Your story.

Your *real*.

When the witch wakes, she begins to take back all the parts of her that have been dis-membered, put in the dark and labelled as taboo.

She re-members.

She realizes that nothing needs fixing. She realizes that her womb is a potent power source, and that she is whole.

She's rooted.

And she's ready to rise.

Reclaim the witch.

Reclaim YOUR power.

Chapter 6

The Witch Wound

Re-membering Your Dis-membered Parts

*'For a woman to actually repossess herself and
to centre, there is a monumental task, taking
years of difficult, painstaking work...*

*Once a woman has done the work of
remembering herself, she is much more
able to change the world effectively.'*

— Vicki Noble, *Shakti Woman*

Re-Member Your Dis-Membered Parts

I was talking with a friend recently and discussing how – despite us both doing so much work on ourselves, and despite everything we know, teach and share – we *still* get triggered by other women. We get triggered by social media and by societal beliefs; and when we witness that triggering, our instant reaction is to berate ourselves – to pick up a stick and beat ourselves with it.

See? Patriarchy doesn't have to do ANYTHING.

Well – nothing apart from smoke a fat cigar and continue to make endless money from the insecurities that it's created in us all.

> **We have to realize and remember that it's
> society that's broken, NOT us. And that
> remembrance has to be a daily practice,
> because the witch wound is cavernous.**

When we re-member, we start to become whole again.

First though, we have to walk *through* the fire; and really believe that it's safe for us to speak, scream, howl, get angry, be loud, cry, curse and even orgasm.

It is safe for you AND for me to do that.

And if it doesn't feel safe? We need to call on others to *help* us feel safe.

If, like so many women, you've felt the burn of a sister betraying or backstabbing you, the work here is to understand the fear and motivation that led her to that place.

For sure, be angry and be mad at her. This is an essential part of the process. But after THAT, I invite you to try finding a place of compassion for her. Because, like you, she's carrying the witch wound – and she's trying to figure all this out too.

We need to make it safe for each other, not by calling each other out and finger pointing, but by calling each other in.

We don't have to agree with each other. We don't even have to like each other a whole lot. That's not the point.

But in order to challenge Patriarchy, create change and begin to heal the witch wound, we DO have to support other women who dare to speak their truth.

Even if it's completely different to our own.

It takes bloody courage to stand up as a woman owning your power.

Just ask Joan of Arc. Her mantra *'I'm not afraid. I was born to do this!'* is the battle cry of many an awakening witch who is answering that deep call from her womb.

Joan's magic powers? Insight, trust, devotion and courage.

She wasn't fearless. We'd be fools if we ever thought we could do all of this without feeling *any* fear. But like Joan, you and I must *feel* the fear and answer it with big courage and love.

You must go into the places you've been taught to be afraid of. Because THAT? That's where your power is.

There was no path for Joan, and there's no definite path for us either. The path doesn't yet exist, because we're creating it. In every act of love and courage. And that's both scary AND exhilarating.

We have to practise love and compassion for ourselves *and* for other women when we fuck up (because we inevitably will!) This is new territory for all of us, and we're ALL remembering how to trust ourselves *and* each other.

So be gentle, yeah?

And everything that's going on in the world right now? That's WHY you've heard The Call. That's WHY you're reading this book.

The patriarchal anaesthetic no longer holds the same potency as it has done for the last 3,000 years. That's why the witch in you is waking. And just so you know? There's a really good chance that she's waking up *pissed*.

So what we're currently experiencing – the raping and the pillaging of Mumma Earth and her resources, fracking, deforestation, the disrespect and total disregard for our planet? That's a direct mirror of how Patriarchy has treated the feminine.

That treatment WILL piss an awakened witch off; and when that happens, her very nature is to *do* something about it.

We feel that it's our responsibility to save the world, but actually, our job *isn't* to save the planet. Because honestly? Mumma Earth doesn't need saving.

Instead, what we actually need to worry about is our own actions and behaviours and treatment of her. We need to see them as a reflection of the actions and treatment of women.

The charge of the witch is to save ourselves.

It's to treat ourselves and each other with the respect and grace and honour that the divine feminine requires, because we are all facets of SHE.

We all came from her, and we will all return to her.

And when we feel, heal and save ourselves; we feel, heal and save the world.

Tend to Your Roots. Then Tend to Hers.

That feeling, healing and saving *will* get messy. Of course it will. Transition is always messy. But there's a reason you're here, this lifetime. It's because you can handle it.

And to handle it, you (and all of us) have to get rooted.

In my book *Love Your Lady Landscape*, I talk about how we have to root to rise. And when I invite you to root, I mean root in ALL the ways. I mean...

Know your roots: know where you came from – your familial and ancestral roots, and how they've shaped you, your beliefs and how you show up in the world.

As a white European woman, I was interested to hear Starhawk – a witch, activist and the author of *The Spiral Dance* – share these powerful words:

'White people can't heal until they come to terms with the witch persecutions. The brutal murder of women in European history has separated those of us with that heritage from our indigenous roots.'

She's right. She's so bloody right.

Know yourself: know ALL the parts. The dark, the angry, the judge-y, the spiritual, the truthful, the uplifting, the silly, the giggly, the painful, the sexual, the trapped, the stifled, the loving, the scared and the sacred parts.

Know them ALL.

Own them all.

When I talk of feeling safe, the REAL safety comes from knowing yourself and all your parts so intimately that NO one can ever 'have' anything on, or over you. When you have fierce self-belief, no one can blame, shame or make you feel 'less than'.

Know your lady landscape: the pelvic bowl is a witch's most powerful magic-making tool. It's a cauldron, a place where we create, make life and connect directly to source.

Place your hands on your womb space (and if you no longer have a womb, that's okay, the energetic imprint still holds power), on your pussy, on your root. Feel how good it feels to hold that much freakin' power in your hands.

When you root into your pelvic bowl and all the magic and power you hold there, *then* you can begin to tend to the roots of the world.

And the good news? By regularly tending to your own roots, you'll automatically be healing the roots of the sisterhood and the world.

Witch, that's multitasking of the *very* best kind.

✿ Face the Fire ✿

Root tending can create fire. Anger. Fierce and righteous anger. It can feel like a dirty ol' mud-wrestle with Kali Ma, but below are some of the steps I use when I'm facing the fire. Some of these are inspired by my gorgeous friend Kimberley Jones, who writes extensively about women's wealth and the witch wound – it's really good stuff.

So how do you face that fire?

You remember.

You remember that you 'know', deep in your cells. I don't want to tell you *how* to remember; but below are some of the steps I used and still use, when I'm facing the fire:

1. **Acknowledge the witch wound.** It exists. It's a real thing. And its impact will come in many more forms than just the ones I've referred to in this book. Some may be universal, but others you'll have directly experienced in the female body that you're in. Call them up, and declare that they be seen.

2. **Notice how that wound is affecting your life right now.** Is there a truth you're not sharing? A step you're not taking because you're too fear-filled?

Is there something you'd love to do in your life, but you're afraid of how others will react? Are you hiding intuitive hits, gifts and abilities? If so, why?

3. Take a few **deep-down-into-the-womb breaths**. Then take a moment to notice where you feel these fears in your body. Just feel and notice them as physical sensations in your body.

4. **Lay your hand over this place, and send it some big love.** Breathe into the place inside you. Breathe into any sensations. Breathe through any emotions that surface. Don't seek to fix, judge or analyse anything. Just breathe into it.

5. Repeat the mantra: 'I am safe. It is safe for me to be in my body.'

6. **Ask for courage.** Ask for faith. Ask for trust. Ask for your sisters, other SHE-led women who are rising and waking the witch in them, to support you and hold you.

7. **Remember that we're never alone in this.** We might *feel* lonely at different points, but being alone is a choice. We can *choose* no longer to feel alone. We can believe that we've *never* been alone.

    Think of all those women who came before us, who've created the conditions for us now. Think of how many books were burned, and how many voices were squelched. And let *that* be your fuel when you ask for the courage to speak out, tell your truth and express your reality.

8. **Ask the divine mother, goddess, SHE, All That Is.** Ask her to help you feel *all* your fire ignite those flames, and ask her to walk with you.

    Witch, you've got this.

꧁꧂

Call In the Men

Neither my husband Rich, who I call The Viking (he's 6ft 7in, and looks like an extra from *Game of Thrones*), nor I claim to be 'enlightened'. However, we do both know that we're here, right now, together, to support the witch awakening.

And through the writing of *Code Red*, *Love Your Lady Landscape* and this book, *WITCH*, Rich became the embodiment of Patriarchy in human form.

Basically, that meant I was a bit bloody angry at him – a LOT of the time. But thankfully, he was, and is, able to hold it all.

And as I'm editing this, some pretty crazy stuff is going on in the world, socially, politically and environmentally. We both know that we're here to do the work of SHE; and so every day, on waking, he asks, *'What can I do to support you in doing the work you do?'*

THIS is the work of the men right now.

It's not to fight wars. It's not to 'grab pussy'. It's not to stay in the space of a perpetual 'boy' who feels threatened by women reclaiming their power and thinks his toys are being taken away from him. It's not to be scared of a woman's wildness, darkness, shadows and edges either – or to see any of these aspects as threatening or ego-puncturing.

Instead, it's to be able to be *with* that wildness, that darkness and those shadows and edges. To hold space for women to explore, nurture and most importantly, express all those thoughts and support them and love them wholeheartedly as they do.

It's to use their big, beating, pulsating-with-love hearts to ask women what the fuck they can do to support them as they wake.

Here's the deal: I have a LOT of rage.

I'm emotive.

I disturb the peace.

I'm super-sensitive, and I feel it *all*.

These are all traits that Patriarchy has suppressed in women. In me. Yet, they're our total freaking super-powers.

And for a while in our relationship, The Viking really didn't know *how* to be with all my rage.

He was patient, though. He was *so* patient while I worked to unpick exactly what it was that I was angry about. And it was this.

ALL OF THIS.

Everything I've shared in these last few chapters. I've been angry about it since birth.

So many of us have, which is why we've been born in these times. We have to feel, expose and express the mess, anger, frustration and continued fucking injustice and mistreatment of girls and women. Of all of us living now, and of all the women who've gone before us and all who've yet to come.

And so many men *want* to help and support us.

We just need to show them how.

> '*One of the most beautiful things I feel right now, is that you see these amazing, empowered women who are stepping up and really reminding us young men, and men in general, that our role is to let the women lead. And yet, we're their protectors, and we stand side by side; but the women are supposed to lead with their hearts.*'
> – NAHKO BEAR, LEAD SINGER OF NAHKO AND MEDICINE FOR THE PEOPLE,
> SPEAKING ABOUT THE INDIGENOUS WOMEN LEADERS AT STANDING ROCK

It's no coincidence that this book is being written during a time when the current US President is a man who says it's okay to 'grab a pussy'. A man who, after receiving a grilling from a female journalist, said 'there was blood coming out of her…wherever'. A man who regularly turned on female targets throughout his campaign.

That man is the epitome of the Patriarchy, trying desperately to cling onto the old and out-of-date structures that no longer serve us. He's here for one last go-around, to show us EXACTLY what Patriarchy looks like in human form. He's the poster-boy for it.

The good news is that he's making it visible. For so long, this has been bubbling away – unreported and unseen – and now it's rising to the surface. It *has* to be seen, it has to be felt, before it can be healed. It has to be brought out into the light so that we can see how destructive and divisive a force it is.

While writing this book, I've felt the very real and true threat of what it is to tell my truth. You may not have been drowned or burned at the stake in a previous life. You may not even believe in past lives, but know this: as Patriarchy begins slowly to crumble, it will try desperately to hold on.

And let me tell you, the tricks that it's willing to play in order to survive and suppress women's power are NOT pretty. They mainly involve making sure that our witch wound – the gaping huge gash that Patriarchy has inflicted upon us – NEVER heals.

It's no wonder that, when a woman decides to hear The Call and wake the witch, fear and resistance come to the surface.

But the time is now, and it's a unique time.

It's a time where we might meet with resistance both inside and out; but despite Patriarchy's best efforts, it's no longer okay to denounce us because we're female.

That means conditions are ripe and ready for us to reclaim the witch.

I will no longer be silenced.

I refuse to be the 'good girl'. To feel like it's 'wrong' to get older.

I will express my reality: my pleasure, my pain and my experience direct from my heart and womb. I will act. I will take responsibility because I'm a witch, and witches aren't here to make others feel comfortable.

They're here to show the full spectrum. To show what truth, lived fully, looks and feels like.

It's safe. You're safe. We're safe.

Repeat these words daily like a mantra, because of course, you won't FEEL safe.

This book isn't a meme on social media. It's not a few words of false reassurance that you scroll past without having to take personal responsibility. This is a call AND it's a response.

So, yes, it's bloody scary stuff. These are bloody scary times, and you won't always feel safe.

But we will ALL be safer if we do this together, yeah?

The Witch's Call

This is a call to all the witches. To any woman who gets angry, who aches, who feels pain, who roars, who cries and who howls.

It's a call to any woman who sees herself in the millions of women who've burnt – and are *still* burning – for their defamed womanhood.

> Feel the energy of the witch – the
> repressed feminine magic and power.
> The energy of the wise and wild woman
> who holds the secrets of Mumma Earth –
> her cycles, her rhythms and her nature.
> Know that you're an ancestress of what is to come.
> Bring the witch back to life and into conversation.
> Come together in support of each
> other and not in competition.

This will be what REALLY messes with Patriarchy: women standing together and encouraging each other. And not in a social-media-friendly photo opportunity way either, but by having conscious, brave and real conversations with each other.

By calling each other in, and not calling each other out. By helping each other to put back the pieces, to become whole and to feel fully supported without being judged or shamed in that wholeness.

Remember, reconnect with, re-wild and reclaim what is rightfully yours.

Yourself.

Your truth.

Your voice.

This is *necessary* for both men and women. The entire planet we inhabit needs to learn from Patriarchy's mistakes; and wake up, listen to and take action based on the wisdom of the witch.

Remember,
Reconnect with
and Reclaim
what is rightfully yours.

Chapter 7

Witch, Please

*Polarities, Contradictions,
Truth and Edges*

I don't want to tell you HOW to be a witch.

If that's what you need, there are a gazillion 'Witchcraft 101' books out there.

But if you:

- Feel your current skin and ways of being are shedding...

- Crave more than anything to live in your body, and to hear and honour her wisdom...

- Are done with playing by the rules, and being told what to do/ wear/say/feel...

- Are done with seeking approval and/or trying to convince others (all of which have been traps to stop you from claiming your natural, spiritual authority)...

... well, I can *definitely* help with that.

Say the word 'witch'.

Give it space to sit in your mouth. Let it move around your body.

Let it grow bolder and stronger in you as you give it space.

Say it out loud.

> ## The true name of a thing is the greatest power you can have. And to call yourself by your true name is the GREATEST empowerment.

Imagine introducing yourself to someone new as a witch. How would that feel?

In a workshop recently, a woman said how much comfier she felt calling herself a 'healer' rather than a witch.

In fact, as she said the word 'witch' to the circle of women who'd gathered, she physically recoiled.

She said it was the visceral power of the word that bothered her. The way people viewed a healer, she believed, was much 'softer' and more inclusive compared to how they perceived a witch.

And while she knew deep in her heart that ultimately, a witch is a healer aligned with Mumma Earth? It was still much easier and far more acceptable to say the word 'healer' than it was to say 'witch'.

She said that 'witch' seemed dark; and that it didn't feel comfortable. It felt painful, in fact.

And this? THIS is the point.

A witch *does* have a relationship with the dark. She's intimately familiar with her shadows because she KNOWS that the only way that we, as women, will ever be fully whole is by acknowledging the dark.

We need to acknowledge our own darkness, without being afraid of it.

I get it. Of course I do. I'm a woman who's been called a 'witch' as an insult. Yet, when you know the power of the word – the potency of woman held within it – you start to get really passionate about claiming it back.

It's going to take practice. Lots of practice. But in reclaiming the word 'witch', you claim your authority. You claim your *power*.

The Witch as a Commodity

At the other end of the spectrum, there are others who use the word 'witch' in a super easy-breezy, watch-how-easily-it-rolls-off-my-tongue way. Using it as a fashionable term, in the same way they use the word 'Gypsy'.

Fashion magazines dedicate entire twelve-page shoots to vamp lipstick, with crushed velvet and black-and-white photography. While artfully curated Instagram feeds are filled with mini-cauldrons, tarot cards and selected herbs.

There are entire websites dedicated to 'modern witches'; and if I'm honest, for a while there, all of that? Well, it really pissed me off.

Being a witch is my belief system. It's my heritage – my way of life. It's who I am at my roots. How could these girls and women trivialize it without feeling the pain and power associated with it?

Then after one of *many* late-night, candle-lit Skype conversations with my coven sister, I realized something. (Wait, you didn't think I had all this stuff figured out, did you?)

I realized that while self-sourcing and trusting ourselves and our inner knowledge are key components of becoming a witch who is awake, we're also *all* desperately trying to figure out how to gain each other's trust again. We're all trying to be visible in a world that Patriarchy has tried to erase us from. We're trying to collaborate from a real place of truth.

And well…that shit takes time. And an open heart. And fellow woken witches who are willing to hold space for you as you try to feel into, explore and navigate it all.

The good news is, I finally got to a place of being really bloody grateful.

I realized how *incredible* it is to be living in a time and place where these girls and women can actually use the word 'witch' in social media memes without fear of repercussion.

That said, I also know that the very nature of the word 'witch' and the power attached to it mean that you simply cannot use it without experiencing something. You just can't.

So if you're NOT taking responsibility for how you use it and what it represents? There's a really good chance (that is, 'a 100 per cent certainty') that you'll get your arse kicked in some way, shape or form.

Reclamation and Reverence

To reclaim the witch in you and show complete reverence for all that SHE is, we all need to:

Dive into the stories of women who inspire you and captivate you – real and fictional, historical and present-day – and get geeky about them. Go read about them, watch movies about them and read their works. Explore the mysteries of who they are, who you are, who we are and what we're made of.

Invite them to join your coven: a coven of women – real or imagined, alive or dead – that you can go to in your journal, in meditation or during dreamtime to seek counsel.

My personal coven includes Anaïs Nin, Florence Welch, Mary Magdalene, Joan Jett, Meggan Watterson, Sybil Leek, Audrey Hepburn, Lady Gaga, Sarah Durham Wilson, Kali Ma, Frida Kahlo, Rizzo from the movie Grease and Dr Christiane Northrup.

Bow at the feet of our foremothers. Recognize the women who have gone before us, and who have made it possible for us to have this conversation, and for me to write this book.

Acknowledge the elders and visionaries of women's spirituality: Luisah Teish, Brook Medicine Eagle, Starhawk, Vajra Ma and Vicki Noble.

Re-member.

Re-member Her Stories and His Stories.

I want you to dig deep. I want you to reconnect with the truth. I want you to feel it, deep in your roots; and I want you to unearth it ALL.

Face the polarities, the contradictions and the inconsistencies between the telling of our stories and our current lived experience.

Really explore the tales you've been told about *who* you should be, *how* you should be and *what* you should be. Unearth and shine light on every way you've ever been disconnected, dis-embodied, dis-eased and dis-membered.

Strip them off, one by one, like the goddess Inanna did as she descended into the Under World. There's a chance that doing this may get a little dark as you dig deep. But that's okay. We're not afraid of the dark any more, remember?

And then, like Inanna on her ascent (because it's ALL cyclic, and you can always come back to the light), decide what still fits, what you want to keep and what you no longer need.

Then the blame game stops here.

Radical Self-responsibility

Yes, we can get angry at the patriarchal structures that mean the odds are never in our favour. Yes, we can get pissed at the continuing attempts of decision-makers and politicians to ignore, disrespect and erase our life-giving super-powers as women. Yes, we can, will and *should* take a stand.

But there comes a time – a pivotal moment – where you have to stop blaming Patriarchy.

Instead, you need to witness how we got to this place, know it and fully understand it.

You need to witness that the pain you feel in acknowledging and daring to step up and heal the wounds of the feminine is an invitation to respond, not react.

You need to witness that your previous lack of self-belief and self-worth, your nagging 'not good enough' voice (or however patriarchal conditioning has shown up in YOUR life) can be reversed.

And then – and this is the work – you need to take fierce and radical self-responsibility.

How?

By claiming back your natural Goddess-given authority and SHE power for ALL of our sakes.

Wake the witch.

The witch is she who looks inward for knowledge, not out. It's she who trusts and respects herself, and she who is whole. (Remembering that whole doesn't mean having it all figured out, far from it).

When you wake *that* witch, you restore your feminine ways. You re-wild, and you become really comfortable with not knowing. You change everything forever and ever and you will never again be who you were before.

You realize you've got work to do – witch work. You've got art to make, people to heal, roots to tend to, humans to create, houses to build, networks to construct, rituals to craft, stories to write, magic to manifest and revolutions to start.

> **You remember you're
> a freakin' badass witch
> woman whose pussy is her
> power source; and whose
> heart will heal us all.**

The 'Wake the Witch' Project

What comes next is the 'Wake the Witch' Project.

It's a bit like the Blair Witch Project but without the snotty noses, bad camera angles and rubbish lighting. (So NOTHING like the Blair Witch Project at all.)

It is, however, everything I've gathered from my own experience, along with insights from my own Book of Shadows, and my personal blend of witches' brew – medicine that has helped me on my own path. Together, they may help you with your own reclamation.

Many of the things that I want to share with you about being a witch are difficult to put into words. I don't want to condense anything or trivialize it; and the way of the witch means that your experiences? Well, they usually just cannot be articulated. After all, they're just that: experiences that are deeply personal to the witch that they happen to.

Which is why, with my pointer finger (just as powerful as *any* wand), I'm drawing a five-pointed pentagram in the air. It's the universal symbol of the witch, and one you'll find when you cut through the centre of an apple – you know, the fruit that Eve was banished from Eden for eating. NO coincidence, right? And at each point of the pentagram, I'm calling in a powerful witch archetype/role/energy/guide-ess to help me share:

The Force of Nature: SHE who cannot be controlled

The Creatrix: SHE who dreams, manifests and makes magic

The Oracle: SHE who trusts her intuition and sees all things

The Healer: SHE who heals herself and heals the world

The Sorceress: SHE who is charmed, dangerous and not afraid of the dark

Now THESE are the kind of witches that girls *should* dress up as at Halloween.

They are five witch entities – archetypes – that are present in each and every one of us.

And experiencing and feeling them fully will wake the witch in EVERY woman.

Of course SHE has many, many features, facets, aspects and faces. But the five I share here have all, at one point in the story of woman, been revered, honoured and necessary.

I share them as a broomstick-prod to your pussy, a wand-wave over your heart, and a stirring of your cauldron. I share them to help you remember. I share them to wake the witch in you.

Some of them will have similarities, while others will totally contradict each other.

Some will make you uncomfy, and others will sing to your soul.

This is the way of the witch. Polarities. Contradictions. Truth and edges. Circles and seasons. You may be called to one specific aspect more than another, and that's okay. Follow and trust your knowing.

I invite you to explore and get curious about each of them. Knowing that each of these facets of the witch is ready to reveal itself to you – to be re-discovered and re-membered within you – will help us ALL to come to a place of wholeness.

We'll re-member our power. And we'll re-discover our own innate badass-ery.

Remember: you
are never alone.

I'm here holding
you. I offer you my
trees, my oceans
and all my beauty.

– Mother Nature

#WAKETHEWITCHES

Chapter 8

The Force of Nature

SHE Who Cannot Be Controlled

A force of nature is a natural phenomenon that cannot be controlled.

YOU, woman, are a force of nature.
You are a natural phenomenon. You are SHE who cannot be controlled.

Can I get a high five for that?

Before you even think about casting a spell, raising energy and making magic, it's important to grow strong, firm roots – deep into the truth of who you are.

And that truth is this: our bodies, if we let them, are deeply in tune with the cycles of the seasons, the elements and the moon.

I am Her and SHE is me.

Yep, what happens in Mumma Nature is mirrored in our own bodies through life and death, menarche and menopause, giving birth, the menstrual cycle and the phases of womanhood.

In fact, our menstrual cycle is the most incredible form of witchcraft there is (there's more on that on page 138). It's our internal monthly map that reflects the phases of the moon and the seasons of nature. Our cyclic nature is our very own personal timekeeper that gives us direction and guidance on everything we do.

We're cyclic, and when we let our cyclic nature be our guide, we can really understand why, for so long, we've felt like we don't fit in or that we don't belong.

Unfortunately, our roots have been pulled away from Mumma Nature.

We eat fruit out of season, and we plan our rest time in the form of one- or two-week holidays and weekend getaways. We even take synthetic hormones to 'manage' our monthly cycles. We try to replace those cycles with control and sameness, instead of recognizing them as our power source.

After all, it's our cyclic natures and direct relationships with Mumma Earth that make us – make YOU – a force that simply cannot be controlled.

They've tried. Oh my goddess, they've tried.

I speak about this a lot in my book *Love Your Lady Landscape* – about how Patriarchy makes it as tricky as possible – biggest freakin' understatement EVER – for us as women to navigate the straight lines that have been created specifically to favour the dudes.

But you ARE a woman.

A woman who's NOT consistent. A woman who ebbs and flows – mentally, emotionally and physically – each month. And as a witch – no pressure – it's your job to return to the ways of the Earth, the cycles and the seasons with complete remembrance and reverence.

It's your job to bring harmony and balance back to *all* stages and cycles of being a woman: the death and the dying, the aging and the letting go, the doing and the being. You need to make sure that they're all being honoured and respected.

When we attune to *all* the ways in which cycles are shown to us, we come into right relationship with both our outer and inner lady landscape.

We realize that we're not separate after all. Instead, we're interwoven; and the wisdom of Mumma Earth flows through each and every one of us.

The Witch's Wheel of the Year

Being connected to the cycles of the Earth is an integral part of being a witch.

How do we navigate the outer and inner landscape of our lives?

How do we feel our way as human beings on the planet?

For thousands of years, the Ancients knew the importance of balance and its sacred pattern. In some seasons, the light is prominent and celebrated. In others, the dark is honoured.

Every nature-based culture, from the ancient Celtic people in the Northern hemisphere to the Aboriginal people in the Southern Hemisphere, celebrated and marked the cyclic wheel of the year. We need to remember our roots, as they continue to affect us today – even though, for the most part, we're completely unaware of it.

As we bring attention and awareness to the cyclic pattern of light to dark and back again, we also adjust to a process that can support our own lives unfolding.

The 'witch's wheel', an annual cycle based in the Celtic tradition, is used by witches around the world to celebrate the Sabbats.

Sabbats are markers of time that are spaced evenly throughout the year, which acknowledge and celebrate agricultural and astronomical events. Personally, I work with the Celtic Calendar: I live in the UK, and that calendar plugs me into the motherboard.

However, it's also a calendar that many witches and Wiccans work with; and it's a great way to nod to, navigate and work with the energies of each season.

The Sabbats

The following table shows the Sabbats in the Celtic Wheel of the Year:

	Northern Hemisphere	Southern Hemisphere
Samhain	October 31	April 30/May 1
Winter Solstice/Yule	December 21/22	June 21
Imbolc/Bride	February 2	August 1
Spring Equinox/ Ostara	March 21/22	September 21/22
Beltane	May 1	October 31/ November 1
Summer Solstice/Litha	June 21/22	December 21/22
Lughnasadh/Lammas	July 31/August 1	February 1/2
Autumnal Equinox/ Mabon	September 21/22	March 21

The Solar Festivals celebrate the height of each season, and are determined by where the sun is in relation to the Earth. This means that dates for each of these will vary from year to year.

The Solar Festivals are:

- Spring Equinox

- Summer Solstice

- Autumn Equinox

- Winter Solstice

The ancient Celtic Fire Festivals mark the gateways into each season; and are often viewed as the high points of the seasonal energy – the times when ritual bonfires were lit. They occur halfway between the Solstices and the Equinoxes; and are sometimes known as Cross-Quarter Days.

These Cross-Quarter Days or Fire Festivals are:

- Imbolc/Bride

- Beltane

- Lughnasadh/Lammas

- Samhain

I invite you to learn what you can about the myths, legends, beliefs and festivals of the land you currently live in. They'll help you to tune in to the natural energies as perceived by the inhabitants of your land through seasons and time. I use the Sabbats as markers to help me work in sync with Mumma Nature all year round.

I'll go through each of the Sabbats in more detail below, and also give you an idea of what I do at each one, so that you can take what works for you and start to craft your own observances and rituals.

Samhain

[End of Oct/beginning of November in the Northern Hemisphere; end of April/beginning of May in the Southern Hemisphere]

The end and the beginning of the Celtic year

Some call it Halloween and others call it All Hallows Eve, but from sundown on 31 October to 1 November, many Pagans and witches refer to the time as Samhain.

What is Samhain?

Samhain (usually said 'sow-en') is an ancient Celtic Fire festival. Much like Mexico's indigenous custom of *Dia de los Muertos*, the Day of the Dead, it focuses on honouring, remembering and paying respect to the Dead – our ancestors who've gone before – through ritual, ceremony and celebration.

Samhain marks the descent of Winter. The leaves are falling from the trees, and life is being drawn away from the surface of the Earth, descending deep into Mumma Earth.

Mumma Earth, for her part, prepares for a winter sleep and draws her energy inwards.

This is a time for introspection; and I invite you to use this season to draw your own energy in and prepare for Winter.

In most places in the Northern hemisphere, Samhain represents the end of the growing season. The frost kills off vegetation, and there is death: an ending.

Many witches and Pagans believe that this ending is when the veil between the worlds of the living and the dead is at its thinnest, making it possible to contact and communicate with our ancestors.

For those who've experienced the death of loved ones in the past year, a Samhain ritual can be an opportunity to bring closure to grieving. It can also help them to adjust to their loved ones being in the Otherworld, by communicating with them.

There are many Samhain rites to celebrate, communicate with and honour the Dead. Here are three that I observe.

⤳ Make an Ancestors' Altar ⤳

I have an everyday, working altar that I sit at, pray to and work spells on (you can find out how to make one of those on page 164), At Samhain, though, I create a special altar dedicated to my ancestors.

I gather photographs, items and souvenirs of deceased family members, friends or pets. Then I arrange the items on a table, and light candles in the memory of those I've lost. I offer each of them a small libation. For example, my nan loved a cup of milky white tea, my dad a cold beer, and my mum loved a Black Russian (an alcoholic drink).

While I arrange the altar, I speak their names out loud, express well wishes and thank them for being part of my life and lineage.

If you're making your altar with other people, invite them to do the same and share stories of those who've passed.

If you're on your own, sit with your ancestors and see what comes through.

⤳ Be Reflective ⤳

Look back on your life over the past year.

Take a look through your journals, at photographs you've taken and anything else you've created over the year. Think about how you've grown, what you've achieved, the challenges you've faced, the adventures you've had, the old friends you've lost and the new ones you've made.

Journal all these things out, or create a mood board or a piece of art that reflects you and the year that has just passed.

Reflecting in this way helps you to move forward with gratitude, have compassion for everything you've dealt with and celebrate all that you are.

⤳ Burn, Baby, Burn ⤳

Write a list of everything you want to let go of – people, experiences, challenges and habits. Then cast that list into the Samhain flames, allowing it all to be burned into ashes.

Circle the fire clockwise, and visualize yourself rising from the flames: new, energized and revitalized, ready for the year ahead.

Now – and this is my favourite part – use tarot, runes, scrying or your favourite method of divination to seek guidance for the year to come.

Write down any messages, symbols or insight you receive to help guide you through the coming year.

◦◦ᦒ◦

Symbols for Samhain

Acorn: It's said that during the Burning Times, giving someone an acorn was a secret nod and a wink to let them know you were a witch. Acorns are symbols of protection, fertility, growth and friendship. They're also given as amulets of good luck and fortune for the year ahead.

Besom (Broom): Practically, a besom is used at Samhain to sweep away the last of the Autumn leaves; but it's also used ritually to sweep out old energy and create space for the new.

The Viking and I made a besom together in 2012 at Samhain so we could sweep away anything we wanted to let go of at the wedding (we married at Yule that year). Then we jumped over the same besom at our handfasting in May the following year.

You can make a besom by gathering a large bundle of twigs and branches, and tying them together tightly. Then create a broom handle from a strong branch, and push it into the middle of the bundle.

I decorated our besom with ribbons and flowers; but you can also make a 'working' besom to keep by your front door for good luck and to ritually cleanse your doorway.

Cauldron: A cauldron is not just a left-over movie prop from every witch movie ever made. It's a practical tool, and one that's closely associated with Samhain.

A cauldron is also feminine. I talk often about how a woman's pelvic bowl is her very own internal witch's cauldron: it's the place where lady magic is created, where feelings, emotions and thoughts are alchemized and it's the cosmic container for all life, death, transformation and rebirth.

Herbs for Samhain

Rosemary: remembrance, protection, purification

Sage: wisdom, wish manifestation, purification

Altar Items for Samhain

Apples; bones; dark crystals; photographs of loved ones; pumpkins; seeds of any kind

The Winter Solstice: Yule

[December 20–23 in the Northern Hemisphere; June 20–23 in the Southern Hemisphere]

Festival of rebirth, midwinter, the shortest day and longest night of the year

Yule holds a special magic for me: it's when I 'officially' married the Viking. We got married on 21 December 2012 because Winter Solstice marks the shortest day and the longest night of the year. It's when we're reminded that no matter how dark it gets, the light ALWAYS returns.

As dark as it is, Yule is also a time of rebirth. Light and life are seen to be returning and conquering death.

Yule represents the time of the first planted seed, the return of the sun and a promise that everything will begin to grow again. It's a turning point – a point of change – where the tides of the year turn and begin to flow in the opposite direction.

Many of us put up a fir tree for Yule because it's evergreen, representing everlasting life amidst the death and darkness. However, if you want to do this, can I ask you to consider honouring a living tree – either in a pot that you bring inside, or outdoors in the earth – rather than cutting a live one down to have in your house for a week, please?

The Yule Log

Not just a chocolate cake, the Yule log was actually originally a large oak log. People would ceremonially bring it into the house and set fire to it at dusk on the night of Yule, lighting it with a branch from the previous year's Yule log.

It's said that once the log is lit, it should burn until it's deliberately extinguished. Allowing it to burn out is considered bad luck.

In England, it's also considered unlucky to buy the Yule log from a shop. It needs be acquired using other means without money changing hands.

The ashes from the Yule log were often used to make protective, healing or fertilizing charms, or scattered over the fields. In Brittany, the ashes were thrown into wells to purify the water, and in Italy they were used as charms against hailstones.

If you're like me, and you live in a house without a fireplace, keeping a branch from last year's log and finding a new oak log to burn each Yule can prove a little tricky. To get around this, the Viking and I wrap up warm, go out into the garden, make jacket potatoes in our fire pit and burn a small log from the tree in our garden.

We both make wishes into the flames, share food, and then when the ashes are cool enough to be safe, I collect some of them in a jar to use in spells – then scatter the rest over my little herb garden.

∾ CANDLE MAGIC ∽

Candles, fire and light are all perfect for making magic at Yule. This simple ritual will prepare you for the new beginnings that are on their way.

What you'll need:

A white candle that can be burned for seven days. You can get these already marked, or you can buy a chunky pillar candle and mark it into seven sections with a sharpie pen, or carve the marks with your athame (see page 152) or a knife.

Incense or sage smudge

Charcoal and fireproof burner

Loose herbs:

- Thyme for courage
- Marjoram, lavender and/or hawthorn for happiness
- Basil, garlic or mint for banishing darkness

What to do:

Begin 12 hours before the Winter Solstice. Prepare yourself and your sacred space with incense, spray or smudge for purification. (Find out how to do this on page 162).

Spend some time being still while you call on your spirit guides to stand beside you to support you.

Light the charcoal and add the herbs.

Light the candle and meditate on the light. Let your gaze be soft, your lids heavy, and focus your eyes on the light of the candle. Notice what your experience is, and how you feel.

Repeat this affirmation:

I am strong.

I am light-filled.

There is abundance in the world, and I shall receive all that I need.

Snuff the candle when one seventh of it has burned. Once you've finished this practice, take out your journal and write whatever comes through for you.

Do this every day until the candle is completely consumed.

⌒⌒⌒

Symbols for Yule

Holly: Bringing holly into your home at Yule symbolizes that you're allowing nature spirits to share your home during the harsh, cold season.

Wreath: The Wheel of the Year is often symbolized as a wreath made from evergreens and placed on your front door.

Wreaths have been used in this way for over 4,000 years. A wreath's circle has no beginning and no end: everything comes back to its point of origin and travels onward again, over and over again.

Herbs for Yule

Ash: a herb of the sun, ash brings light into your home at the Winter Solstice.

Frankincense: sacred to the sun god Ra, frankincense is burned in rites of purification and protection. Burning it as incense is a great way to call in the light at Yule.

Altar Items for Yule

Antlers; anything that represents the sun; cloves; mistletoe; red, green or white crystals; wreaths (symbolic of the Wheel of the Year)

Imbolc or Bride – 2 February

[End of January/beginning of February in the Northern Hemisphere; end of July/beginning of August in the Southern Hemisphere]

The Earth's awakening

Pagans celebrate the Festival of Imbolc or Bride around 2 February; and Christians celebrate the same date, but call it Candlemas.

Imbolc is an Irish-Gaelic word that's translated variously as 'in the belly' and 'ewe's milk'. It represents the quickening of light and life. The first sprouting of leaves can be seen, and we celebrate the successful passing of winter and the beginning of the agricultural year.

It's also a day of celebrating the Celtic Goddess Brigid (sometimes known as *Bride*, which is usually pronounced 'briydee'). Brigid is the Goddess of Poetry, Healing, Smithcraft and Midwifery. If you can make it with your hands, Brigid rules it.

She's a triple Goddess, so on this day we honour her in all her aspects. We welcome the Goddess who has been renewed in the winter and reborn as the Flower Maiden. She has passed through Her phase as the Hag, Crone or Wise One, and is a Maiden again.

This is a time for communing with Brigid, and lighting her sacred flame. This flame was once marked in Europe with huge blazes, torches and fire in every form.

The fire represents the spark of illumination and inspiration that burns in our bellies, and encourages us to create and make. What was born at the Solstice begins to manifest now, which means we each light our own light, and set ourselves tasks and challenges. We nurture and kindle our resolutions, and begin to look outwards again and perform outer activity – although first, we look deep within ourselves to discover what potential lies there, waiting to be fulfilled.

DEVELOPING YOUR WITCHY POWERS

Psychometry is a psychic skill that helps you to pick up information from an inanimate object. With practice, you can accurately describe someone's characteristics, their physical appearance or experiences they've had just by holding an item that they've owned or worn a lot, like a watch or a necklace.

Start with an object from someone you know.

Hold the object in your left hand and see what impressions you can pick up. You might get words, names, images, sensations or colours.

Then ask a friend to give you an item from someone *they* know, do the same and ask for their feedback.

As you start to practise, keep a diary of what certain colours mean to you – perhaps when you see yellow, it means the person who owned the item had a vibrant and outgoing personality.

As you practise with different items, you'll start to see patterns emerge.

Welcome the Sun

The passing of Winter and emergence of Spring is a great time for initiations.

At Imbolc, it's traditional to turn on every light in the house, even if it's only for a few moments. Or you could light a candle in each room in honour of the sun's rebirth.

If snow is on the ground, walk in it for a moment and remember the warmth of Summer. Then, with your dominant hand (the one you write with), trace an image of the sun in the snow.

Symbols for Imbolc/Bride

Brigid's Cross: This is a traditional fire wheel symbol, found at the hearths of homes throughout Ireland, and now worldwide, as a symbol of protection.

Brigid Doll: A very old tradition involves making a Brigid doll, which can then be included in a ceremony and/or placed in 'Bride's Bed' to bring fertility and good fortune to the home.

Flame: Imbolc is a Fire Festival, and fire of all kinds is associated with Brigid: the fire of creativity, the protective hearth fire, and her fire wheel – Brigid's Cross – which heralds her as a sun goddess.

Serpent: In Celtic mythology, Brigid was associated with a hibernating serpent that emerged from its lair at Imbolc. Traditionally, serpents were associated with creativity and inspiration – as well as the powerful Kundalini energy of the Eastern Mysteries.

Paths of Earth energy (sometimes called ley lines) were also called serpent paths; and at Imbolc, they stir from their slumber.

Herbs for Imbolc

Blackberry: sacred to Brigid, blackberry leaves and berries are used to attract prosperity and healing. This is a Goddess plant, belonging to the planetary sphere of Venus.

Coltsfoot: Coltsfoot or 'sponnc' (Gaelic) is a herb associated with Brigid. It's a herb of Venus that moves emotional and physical stagnation, and is used magically to engender love and bring peace.

Ginger: this herb revitalizes and stimulates the 'fire within'. It also helps to align you with the rise of Kundalini serpent energy at this time of year!

Altar Items for Imbolc

Brigid's cross; candles (especially green candles); pen/paper; representations of the maiden/youth; swan feathers; vision boards; white and blue flowers and crystals

Ostara: the Spring Equinox

[March 20–23 in the Northern Hemisphere; September 20–23 in the Southern Hemisphere]

The first day of Spring, day and night are equal

This festival is named after the Anglo-Saxon Goddess Eostre or Eastre, also known in Old German as Ostara. Little is known about this goddess, except that her festival was celebrated at the Spring Equinox, which became Easter; that she was a goddess of fertility; and that she was connected with hares and eggs.

The Equinox is a time both of fertility and new life, and of balance and harmony. Light and dark are here in balance, but the light is growing stronger.

It's also a time of birth and of manifestation. Daffodils, tulips and crocuses are all in full bloom, blossom appears on trees and catkins can be found on hazel and willow trees.

Because Equinox is a time of growth and balance, it's a good time to work on balancing yourself and the subtle energies within you: chakras, masculine and feminine qualities and the light and dark aspects.

ᴄᴏ Egg Magic ᴄᴏ

Grab an egg – the symbol of fertility and rebirth (see page 124) – and write, sing or whisper your wishes and intentions into it. Your goal lives within you in the same way that creation lives within the egg; and like the egg, your goal has everything it needs to manifest.

Then draw two interlocking triangles to form a six-pointed star on your egg. This star symbolizes one of the most important keys in magic: as above, so below. Whatever you can create in your imagination, you can manifest on the physical plane.

Now bury the egg in Mumma Nature, and ask her to hold, nurture and help you to bring your wishes into being.

The Viking and I do this every year, and we bury our eggs under my matrilineal rose bush in the back garden for extra SHE juju.

ᴄᴏ Ostara Honey Cakes ᴄᴏ

The best witches know that a Sabbat is the perfect reason to eat, drink and be merry. Why do you think there are eight Sabbats?

I've only just started to collect recipes for all my favourite Sabbat-based treats, but I want to share this one with you because every Ostara-time, my nanna would make Honey Cakes. And now, every Ostara I make them too. (Except I add wine, because…well, I like wine.)

What you'll need:

125ml/4fl oz/½ cup Riesling wine
1 egg
65g/2¾oz/⅔ cup plain flour
340g/11¾oz/1 cup honey
2 tbsp sugar
⅛ tsp cinnamon
⅛ tsp nutmeg
Dash of salt

What to do:

Beat the egg together with the wine in a bowl.

In another mixing bowl, sift together the flour, cinnamon, sugar and salt.

Add the flour mixture to the egg mixture and stir until blended into a smooth batter.

Let it sit for 30 minutes.

In another small bowl, mix the honey and nutmeg.

In a skillet, heat up about a 1cm/½ inch of coconut oil. Drop 1 tbsp batter into the oil, and fry until golden brown.

Drain off the oil, and dip the cake into the honey mixture.

Symbols for Ostara

Eggs: The egg is a symbol of rebirth. Its yolk represents the sun, and its white represents the Goddess. Egg production in hens is stimulated when the bird's retina is stimulated by more than 12 hours of light, therefore more eggs are produced after the Equinox.

You can use eggs to create talismans, or ritually eat them.

Lamb: The lamb was sacred to virtually all the virgin goddesses of Europe, the Middle East and Africa.

Rabbits and hares: Rabbits are symbols of fertility because of their amazing rate of reproduction. The rabbit is also the lunar hare, sacred to the Moon Goddess.

In the West, the hare – like the cat – was a common witch's familiar; and witches were said to have the power to turn themselves into hares. My nanna used to say that women weren't allowed to eat hare, because eating a hare was like eating your grandmother. True-ish fact!

Herbs for Ostara

Lemongrass: this herb is cleansing, and can be used to clarify communication with the opposite sex. Make it into a tea to drink at Ostara to clear the way for new opportunities.

Spearmint: carry a spearmint leaf for healing, or use this herb in a ritual bath to help you feel vital and frisky.

My nanna once told me that you should write a wish on paper and wrap it in spearmint leaves. Then put the spearmint-wrapped wish in a red cloth, sew it into a little package with some red thread, and keep it safe and secret.

When the scent of the spearmint is gone, your wish should apparently come true.

Try it and let me know if it works. I've never done it, but writing this makes me want to give it a go.

Altar Items for Ostara

Amethyst crystals; baskets; eggs; feathers; flowers; seeds; honey cakes; soft wool or cloth

Beltane

[End of April/beginning of May in the Northern Hemisphere; end of October/beginning of November in the Southern Hemisphere]

Heralding Summer,
festival of fertility

Beltane (also spelled Bealteinne, Bealtaine and various other ways) is the beginning of the Celtic Summer: the light season of the year. Like Samhain, it's a time when the veil between the worlds is thin – a time to communicate with spirits, particularly nature spirits.

People would traditionally build fires at Beltane, then jump over the flames. Young, unmarried people would leap the bonfire and wish for a husband or wife. Young women would leap it to ensure their fertility, and couples would leap it to strengthen a bond. (The Viking and I did this at our handfasting!)

Celebrate Beltane by taking pleasure in life, by having lots of amazing sex and by enjoying the gifts of nature and the Goddess.

❧ How to Celebrate Beltane ☙

Wash your face in dew at sunrise on Beltane for beauty in the coming year. (Traditionally you'd use the dew from a hawthorn tree, but dew from grass and flowers will do.)

If you live near water, make a garland or posy of spring flowers and cast it into a stream, lake or river to bless the water spirits.

Beltane is one of the three spirit-nights of the year when the faeries can be seen. At dusk, twist a rowan sprig into a ring and look through it; you may see them.

Plaiting and weaving straw, creating things with wicker and making baskets and fabrics are all traditional arts for this turn in the Wheel of the Year. It's also a great time to make and bless a witches' ladder (find out how to make yours on page 172).

❧ Beltane Love Spell ☙

Make this potion under the full moon before Beltane, but wear it like a perfume on the day before, during and after Beltane itself if you want to get smooch-y.

what you'll need:

A white candle
A bowl or chalice
Pure spring water
A rose or clear quartz crystal
A red rose, a pink rose and a white rose
A small bottle
Vodka

what to do:

Cast your circle – preferably outdoors. Or, if you're indoors, next to a window with a view of the full moon. If the weather is bad or cloudy and you can't see the moon, use a candle flame instead.

Hold a bowl or chalice full of pure spring water, and catch the reflection of the moon (or candle flame) in the water.

Call to the Goddess Aphrodite, and ask Her to send Her divine essence flowing into the water along with the moonlight. Concentrate on what perfect love means to you, and instil your own essence into the water by blowing gently on it.

Next, add rose petals and buds to the water. Add a crystal that you've held up to the moonlight and consecrated to a Goddess of Love. A touch of rose or jasmine oil would be nice too, but it's not necessary.

Pour your water into a bottle, and add an equal amount of vodka to seal the potion. Keep this potion in a dark space out of the sunlight for the magical properties of the night to remain potent.

Use this potion to anoint candles and magical workings – especially love spells – and poems. Use it like a perfume to attract a perfect love to you.

ᛞ

Symbols for Beltane

Fire: The bonfire, or balefire, is one of Beltane's oldest traditions and should contain nine sacred woods – oak, hawthorn, birch, elder, ash, rowan, holly, willow and yew.

Light the fire and jump over it with your partner if you're looking to conceive. Women also sometimes wear ashes from the fire in a bag around their necks to aid fertility.

Maypole (or anything phallic, to be honest): This time of year is ALL about sex and fertility. The maypole represents the male, and the ribbons that are danced and wrapped around it represent the female.

Herbs for Beltane

Hawthorn: the classic flower to decorate the Maypole, hawthorn is a herb of fertility used in handfastings and weddings.

Meadowsweet: used in love spells, meadowsweet is also placed in the home to bring peace, joy and love to everyone who lives there or visits.

Altar Items for Beltane

Eggs; lingam/yoni (phallus/vulva) symbols; red and orange crystals; red and white ribbons; red candles; rose petals

Litha: *Summer Solstice*

[June 20–23 in the Northern Hemisphere; December 20–23 in the Southern Hemisphere]

Summer's height, the longest day and the shortest night

At the Summer Solstice, the sun is at its highest and brightest; and the day is at its longest. Flowers are in bloom, ready for pollination and fertilization. Yet, once they're fertilized, they die so that the seeds and fruits may develop, and Summer fruits may appear for a short (but delicious!) season.

June was considered by some to be the luckiest month to be married in, and it's the time of the Mead Moon or Honey Moon. A tradition was for newlyweds to drink mead daily for a month after their wedding, hence the post-wedding holiday being named the honeymoon.

Although the days begin to grow shorter after the Summer Solstice, the time of greatest abundance is still to come.

This is a time of beauty, love, strength, energy, rejoicing in the warmth of the sun and the promise of the fruitfulness to come. It seems a carefree time, yet in the knowledge of life is the knowledge of death, and the fact that beauty is only transitory.

The power of the sun at the Solstice is protective, healing, empowering and revitalizing. It adds a powerful charge to all spells, crystals and herbs; so divination was traditionally practised on this night.

⤳ ELDERFLOWER CHAMPAGNE ⤵

A traditional favourite, elderflowers peak at Midsummer. Pick them in the fullness of a sunny day, ideally on Midsummer's Day.

The elder is sacred to the Mother Goddess, and is often called the Witch's Tree, the Elder Mother or Queen of the Trees. It is protective, with wonderful healing properties. It aids transformation, change and renewal.

What you'll need:

1.2 litres/2 pints water
1.25kg/2¾lb sugar
8 large elderflower heads
4 lemons
4 tbsp mild white wine vinegar

What to do:

NOTE: use screw-top bottles to store your Elderflower Champagne, because this stuff will fizz; and if it's not bottled tightly, it can explode! I keep mine in the garden, just in case.

Before you begin, make sure the elderflowers are clean. You don't want any insects or bugs getting involved.

Boil the water and dissolve the sugar into it.

When the water is cool, add the elderflowers, the juice of two of the lemons and slices of the other two, plus the vinegar.

Cover with a clean cloth and leave for a day.

Strain through a fine sieve or piece of muslin, carefully squeezing the flowers to extract as much flavour as possible.

Store in clean screw-top bottles.

Leave well alone for 10 days or so. Drink within a month. Enjoy and give thanks to the Spirit of the Elder. And to me, for introducing it to you, because it really is SO good.

⟝⟡⟞

Symbols of Litha

Dreamtime: A Midsummer night's dream is said to be one of magic and wonder.

To create a pouch for psychic dreams, put mugwort and bay leaves in a piece of yellow material, sew it up with red thread and place it under your pillow.

(Yep: this is another of nanna's Gypsy spells. I know this one works though, because I've done it myself, and I still do it!)

The Sun: This is the Summer Solstice, so it makes total sense that the symbol of Litha is the sun. The sun is at its fullest on this day, so try to make sure you soak up as many of its rays as possible.

(If there's cloud, use your imagination and/or wear yellow clothes or accessories.)

Herbs of Litha

Lavender: a masculine healing herb, lavender was thrown onto the Midsummer ritual fires as a sacrifice to the gods.

St John's wort: if St. John's wort is picked on Midsummer and worn, it's supposed to ward off fevers and colds. There are some who even say that St. John's wort plucked during Midsummer can make the wearer invincible.

Of course, along with invincibility comes the ability to attract the love and lust of the object of *your* love and lust.

Altar Items for Litha

Mirrors; seashells; summer fruits and flowers; Tiger's eye crystal

Lughnasadh or Lammas

[End of July/beginning of August in the Northern Hemisphere; end of January/beginning of February in the Southern Hemisphere]

Festivals of gratitude and marriage

Lughnasadh or Lammas is celebrated on August eve or August 1, and is the festival of the first harvests. Lammas is the Anglo-Saxon name for the festival, meaning *Loaf mass*. Lughnasadh is the festival of Lugh, a Celtic god of light, fire, crafts and skills.

Lammas is a time of the fullness of life, and a celebration of the bountiful and abundant Mumma Earth. The main themes of Lammas are to give big thanks, high fives and deep bows to the Goddess for Her bountiful harvest, and to state your hopes and intentions for what *you* wish to harvest (Lammas is the very beginning of the harvest), sacrifice or transform.

⤞ Make a Grain Mother ⤝

To make your own Grain Mother or Corn Dolly, you'll need stalks of wheat, oats, barley or rye.

The Viking and I go for a drive in the country and always find stalks left growing on the edges of fields after harvesting. Failing that, any grasses and/or reeds you can find will work.

Let your creativity go wild. If you feel confident, weave your Grain Mother into being; but if that's not your thing, you can just tie her into being with yellow or orange ribbons.

As you weave and tie the ribbons, give thanks for the gifts of your Harvest. Place your Grain Mother on your altar or at the centre of your celebrations.

At Samhain, return the grain stalks to the Earth: they contain the seeds of future harvest.

Symbols of Lammas

Bread: Lammas is also known as The Feast of Bread – the celebration at which the first of the grain harvest is consumed in ritual loaves.

Baking and breaking bread with the people I love at Lammas is my most favourite thing to do (even if I now have to go for the sourdough option, because gluten makes me look six months pregnant. Boo.)

Grapes and wine: Like we need an excuse, right? But grapes are a sacred symbol of abundance; and what better way to give thanks for our abundance than to raise a glass? Make mine a rosé. Thanks.

Herbs of Lammas

Meadowsweet: also known as Queen-Of-The-Meadow, meadowsweet was often worn as a garland for Lammas celebrations, and was a traditional herb for wedding circlets and bouquets at this time of year.

Mint: Mint's magical properties are both protective and healing. Plus, at this stage in the year, its properties of drawing abundance and prosperity are very appropriate. You can wear mint in a medicine bag around your neck, or place a leaf in your purse.

Altar Items for Lammas

Ears of corn; hand-made items and crafts; symbolic representations of our accomplishments; wheat and other grains; yellow and green crystals and flowers

Mabon: The Autumn Equinox

[September 20–23 in the Northern Hemisphere; March 20–23 in the Southern Hemisphere]

Festival of harvest,
when day and night are equal

The two Equinoxes are times of equilibrium. Day and night are equal and the tide of the year flows steadily; but whilst the Spring Equinox manifests the equilibrium *before* action, the Autumn Equinox represents the relaxation that comes after action. It's the time to take satisfaction in the work of the Summer and reap its benefits.

The Autumn Equinox is celebrated on or around 21 September, and is sometimes called 'the Witch's Thanksgiving': a time to appreciate and give thanks to the Goddess for her bounty, and to share in the joys of the harvest.

We celebrate the abundance of the Earth, and we make wine and/or jam from any excess fruit. That way, we can preserve the richness of the fruits of the Earth to give us joy throughout the year.

Mabon marks the completion of the harvest, and the balance of both light and dark and male and female. It also acknowledges the waning power of the sun; and the coming, once again, of the darkness.

Mabon is a good time to cast spells of balance and harmony; and is also a time of change. Protection, wealth and prosperity spells are appropriate as well.

During Mabon, stones ruled by the sun will help to bring its energy to you. Good options include clear quartz, amber, peridot, diamond, gold, citrine, yellow topaz, cat's-eye and aventurine.

⊶ Mabon Magic Hot Apple Cider ⊷

A magical Mabon beverage is hot apple cider. Apple rules the heart, and cider alone is a self-love potion. By spicing it with cinnamon, which is ruled by Jupiter and the sun, we are in essence, ingesting the sunlight.

What you'll need:

960ml/1¾ pints/4 cups apple cider
½ tsp whole cloves
960ml/1¾ pints/4 cups grape juice
cinnamon sticks
1 tsp allspice

What to do:

In a saucepan, heat the cider and grape juice.

Add the cinnamon, allspice and cloves.

Bring to boiling, then lower the heat and simmer for five minutes.

Serve from a cauldron (obviously!).

⊷⊶

Symbols of Mabon

Cornucopia: The word cornucopia is derived from two Latin words: 'cornu', meaning 'horn' and 'copia', meaning 'plenty'.

Place a cornucopia on your personal altar to attract prosperity. Fill it with dried sprigs of sage, rosemary, thyme, mugwort, parsley, and other sacred plants, such as acorns, which are associated with well-being, prosperity, and good fortune.

Dedicate the cornucopia as a tool of abundance, then place deep within it a handwritten wish. Keep the cornucopia in a visible place so that you see it every day.

Take actions that will help your wish come into being. When it has, give thanks by offering the cornucopia contents to a sacred fire or by burying them in the ground.

Divination: The Norse believed that your fate for the coming year was sealed at this time. They performed divination to see whether their life in the past year had been pleasing to the deities. So either throw some runes, or pull a tarot card on the evening of Mabon.

Herbs of Mabon

Benzoin: not only does benzoin relieve stress and anxiety, but it's also good to burn for purification as we enter into the darker months. Add benzoin to cinnamon and basil, and use it as an incense if you're looking to attract customers to your place of business.

Calendula (Marigold): make a green flannel or fabric bag filled with golden calendula flowers, and place it beneath your pillow before you go to sleep. It's said that if you breathe the fragrance of these flowers, you'll make your own luck and fortune for the dark months ahead.

Altar Items for Mabon

Apples; art; berries; gourds; harvest vegetables; maroon and gold items; pinecones; pomegranates; rose quartz and amber crystals

A Final Thought on the Sabbats

There's so much written about the lore, stories, magic and gods and goddesses of each Sabbat that there's no way I could include it all. So consider this simply a stir of the Sabbat cauldron.

What you add to it, and how you choose to celebrate each turn of the wheel, is entirely up to you. But by connecting with Mumma Nature in this way – through herbs, food, magic, ritual and the lore of the land – you reconnect with the rhythms of nature.

And when you recognize how these reflect the pattern of human life, you can start to remember how you are a part of that universal rhythm. You ARE that universal rhythm.

Sigh.

⤳ MAKE A WHEEL OF THE YEAR ↢

Why not make your own Wheel of the Year to remind you of the Sabbats and what you're celebrating; and then start to add in your own rituals and recipes.

Your wheel can be as simple or as fancy as you like: just start by drawing a circle and divide it using eight lines so that it forms a wheel. Label each section with a Sabbat, then colour it and decorate it in a way that feels good.

Let this become YOUR Wheel of the Year. Add any feelings, colours or symbols that feel appropriate too.

(If you do this, please take a picture and share on social media with the hashtag #wakethewitches – I LOVE a creative project!)

Esbats

Esbats are moon rites; and to a witch, they are *just* as important as the Sabbats – they're the time for all magical workings. While the Sabbats are fire and sun festivals to celebrate the changing of the seasons, Esbats are dedicated to the moon in her various phases.

They're a way to honour SHE, the Goddess. These are considered the 'working' celebrations: the time when a witch works to attract, invoke protection, banish or perform spells.

Yep, they're when the witch gets to work!

New Moon Magic

This time is used for personal growth, healing and blessing new projects or ventures. It's also a good time to consecrate new tools and objects you wish to use during rituals, ceremonies or an upcoming festival.

Waxing Moon Magic (First Quarter Moon)

Between the new and full moon is a period of the waxing moon. This time is used for attraction magic, love spells, protection and healing energy for couples.

Full Moon Magic

This time is used to banish unwanted influences in your life. It's also ideal for creating protection magic, performing divination, setting up plans and releasing old patterns or issues.

Full moon magic can be conjured during the three days before the rise of the full moon, the night of the full moon and during the three days afterwards.

Waning Moon Magic (Last Quarter Moon)

Between the full moon and the dark moon is the period of the waning moon. Use it to banish and reject those things that influence you in a negative way. Let go of negative emotions, diseases, ailments and bad habits; and perform special spells for clearing.

Dark Moon Magic

The dark moon period occurs three days before seeing the sliver of the new moon in the sky. This is the time when you can't see the moon in any phase. Typically, no magic is performed during this period: it's time to give yourself a break, turn inwards and replenish your own energies. Vision quests, yoga nidra and deep meditations are great in this phase to help you focus on personal matters, questions and answers.

The Monthly Moons

The rotation of the Earth produces 13 full moons during the year; and each one has a magical name or association. (Note: the moons have many different names depending on the spiritual path/tradition you follow. This is a mashup of what I call them!)

Moon	Month
Wolf Moon	January
Storm Moon	February
Chaste Moon	March
Seed Moon	April
Hare Moon	May
The Long Night's Moon	June
Mead Moon	July
Sturgeon Moon	August
Barley Moon	September
Blood Moon	October
Snow Moon	November
Oak Moon	December
Blue Moon	28-day cycle *

* Blue Moon

This occurs when the full moon appears twice in the same month during its 28-day cycle. This typically occurs in months with 31 days.

It's also called a Goal Moon, and is used to set goals for your life. Use it to acknowledge any mistakes you might have made, and to review lessons that will help you improve your life and set new goals specifically for those issues.

Harvest Moon

This is the Full Moon that appears nearest to the Mabon festival. It can be used specifically to call in favours or to add extra protection.

Moon Mapping

It's a good idea to sit down with your yearly calendar and mark the moon phases and Sabbats for the coming year.

Some witches use Samhain as their New Year, and use this time to prepare for the year ahead. It's well known that I'm a geek for all things cyclic, so I sit down on Samhain, and I write all the Sabbats and Esbats in my diary for the coming year (and then punch them into my online calendar too).

There are also apps that show the moon phases on your online calendar and smartphones, which is total technological witchcraft.

Womb–Moon Phases

The phases of the feminine cycles – life and menstrual – are also aligned with the moon phases: waxing, full, waning and dark. And these, in turn, are also aligned with the seasons of Spring, Summer, Autumn and Winter.

My books *Code Red* and *Love Your Lady Landscape* are both filled with insight and wisdom on the power of our cyclic nature and menstruation. *Briefly* though, here's a quick rundown: the moon cycle has 29½ days, changing from the waxing new moon of increasing light, to the full moon of total illumination, to the dark waning moon of decreasing light, and back to the waxing new moon of increasing light again.

Month after month, the moon cycle mirrors a woman's menstrual cycle, which also has an average length of 29½ days. (I work with women and talk about periods daily, so I KNOW how much this can vary. But for the purpose of THIS conversation, we're keeping it simple!)

And similar to the moon cycle, a woman's menstrual cycle changes from the pre-ovulation of new growth, to the ovulation of full power, to the premenstrual phase of harvest and letting go, and back to menstruation for renewal again.

Menstrual Phase	Goddess Phase	Season Phase	Moon Phase
Pre-ovulation	Maiden	Spring	Waxing moon
Ovulation	Mother	Summer	Full moon
Premenstruation	Wise and wild woman	Autumn	Waning moon
Menstruation	Crone	Winter	Dark moon

Being able to recognize and connect with these cycles and their phases allows us to understand – and most importantly, begin to trust – ourselves, our cyclic nature and the wisdom that comes with it.

> *'If we surrendered to Earth's intelligence we*
> *could rise up, rooted, like trees.'*
> – RAINER MARIA RILKE

Seriously, THIS is magic. Lady Magic.

When you stop trying to work to a straight-line, dude-centric agenda that demands you wake up and do the same thing, day in day out, for an allocated number of hours, and instead tune in to the ebb and flow of:

- Your menstrual cycle

- The current moon phase

- The season

- Your life phase

… you'll experience how you can show up to life, rooted, whole and truthful.

Your family, your work, your relationship, your pleasure will ALL benefit.

This stuff is ancient. Yet right now, it's radical and it's 'bloody' revolutionary to go with the flow.

EVERYTHING is connected.

EVERYTHING is cyclic.

Everything dies so that it can be reborn. Over and over.

Nothing ever truly ends. Every death brings life, and every ending brings a new beginning. It's pretty freakin' incredible, right?

Why is alignment with the Earth and Mumma Nature important?

You'll notice that the more aligned you are with yourself, the more your feminine spirit awakens. And the more aligned you are with your feminine spirit, the more aligned you are with the Earth and her cycles and seasons. After all, nature is the feminine, and your body and the Earth are one.

You are a FORCE OF NATURE.

I am a force of nature.

The 'Wake the Witch' Project

Invoke SHE Who Cannot Be Controlled by:

Heavy seasoning: celebrate and connect with the turning of the wheel – the Solstices, Equinoxes and seasons. Use the rituals I've shared in the book, or create new and personal ones that work for you.

Go with the flow: honour and chart your cyclic nature. Check in with your body rhythms daily and connect with your menstrual cycle: it's an ever-unfolding map to the truth of who you are.

Grow Roots: breathe deep into your womb space for 10 minutes a day. This creates strong, connected roots so you're less likely to feel pressured and manipulated or fall under the spell of the patriarchal constructs that the society we currently live in dictates.

–

Chapter 9

The Creatrix

*SHE Who Dreams,
Manifests and
Makes Magic*

Woman is, was, and always will be a Creatrix.

Write it. Film it. Design it. Publish it.
Crochet it. Sauté it. Whatever, CREATE.

That's my personal take on the original quote by Joss Whedon, but you get the idea, right?

We are *always* creating.

It's what we do.

Diane Stein, author of *All Women Are Healers*, opens her book with *'Women were the creators of the world, the Goddess-birthgivers, the inventors of positive/peaceful civilization.'*

It doesn't matter whether it's creating a life in our womb or an amazing piece of art. Whether it's creating a network of women who speak out against injustice or an incredible aubergine, lentil and coconut curry. Wherever we put our thoughts and energy, we manifest magic. Good and bad.

It's as simple as that.

We can use the magic of our creative power for good, to improve our lives and to create health, abundance and happiness. Or we can moan and groan and create sameness.

Either way, we're *always* creating.

Every word we speak is a spell.

'Abracadabra' is said by some to be Hebrew for 'I create what I speak.' (Not speaking Hebrew myself, I cannot confirm or deny this; but it would be kind of great if it was true, wouldn't it?)

What I DO know is that I've pretty much been a manifesting maven for as long as I can remember – I just didn't know that's what it was called.

My first manifesting experience was when I was seven and on holiday at Butlins (a super-retro holiday camp here in the UK). I was about to take part in a donkey race, and I wanted to win that race more than ANYTHING IN THE WORLD.

(Don't judge me: I was seven!)

I remember crossing my fingers tight and repeating in my head: 'I've won, I've won, I've won.' I kept repeating that phrase until I crossed the finish line and got my hands on that first-place rosette.

So of course, I tried it again. In fact, for the rest of that holiday, it didn't matter what I focused on – fizzy pop, the DJ playing my favourite song without me having to ask, a lion keyring I wanted – if I believed in it hard enough, it *actually* happened.

I felt like Sabrina the Freakin' Teenage Witch.

Of course, since then, I've turned pro.

For example, I get told all the time: 'Lisa, your husband is amazing! Where can I meet one like him?' Or sometimes: 'Does Rich have a brother? He's so lovely!'

You want the truth? I manifested him.

Yep, I manifested a man.

It sounds like a feature straight out of *Cosmopolitan* magazine, right?

And yes, I've heard people mock the power of manifestation because books like *The Secret* make it sound like a cosmic shopping list, where you put in your order and wait for everything you ever desired to be delivered to you.

But for me, manifestation is my most favourite magic.

You see, a few years before Manifesting A Man (and I'm totally trademarking that!), I created a super-simple Make It Happen spell.

I'd used that spell to score a contract for a book I'd pitched. It had helped me to freelance for magazines I loved without having to work in an office. I'd even used it to write a figure of money I wanted to make, and then *made* that money.

So I decided to modify the spell to Manifest A Man.

I waited until the new moon on 11 July 2010.

I lit a candle, whispered some magic words to SHE and got specific.

I wanted to find love. The kind of love you only read about.

I got *really* specific and wrote a list.

Hair colour wasn't important to me, but the fact that he'd support me in my creative dreams was. The clothes he wore didn't concern me, but I wanted a man, not a boy – someone who had the ability to love and be loved in return. (Yes, I'd watched *Moulin Rouge*. It's one of my top five favourite movies EVER.)

I wrote ALL of it down in a love letter to SHE.

Then I made a mojo bag: a little magic bag that I could wear discreetly around my neck for the moon cycle ahead. I filled it with a small rose quartz crystal, a small piece of paper with my wish to find love written on it, various love-inducing herbs and the love potion scent that I'd created at Beltane. (Want to make your own? Instructions are on page 126.)

I placed the list under my pillow, and carried the mojo bag with me every single day.

Then I got to work practically. Every morning in meditation, I'd visualize this man and the things that we'd do together. I asked friends to set me up on dates; and despite my initial trepidation about online dating, I even joined a few dating websites.

I made a few connections online, none of which rocked my world.

I went on a blind date set up by a friend, which was a complete disaster. (He was French and it was Lost in Translation. NOT the movie. It was really ALL lost in translation.)

Then, exactly one moon phase later, at the next new moon, I had a message in my inbox from a man describing himself as an honourable, courageous 6ft 6in Viking. He was masculinity personified.

I tried to play it cool (which lasted approximately five minutes), and I replied.

What happened next was most definitely the stuff of the Hallmark movie channel.

We spent two whole weeks exchanging emails. It felt romantic and decadent, and my heart did double-thumps each time I found a new message from him in my inbox. Other men messaged me too, but I wasn't interested. I knew that this Viking was the one.

When we eventually did meet, under a full moon, he was everything I'd imagined. Our first kiss was on a beach at dusk, and he told me he loved me on our third date. Then, six months later, we moved in together.

I make no apology for how much love and affection that man and I show each other. He has every quality I outlined on my list, and I'm thankful every day that we exist on the same celestial plane and get to do this lifetime together. Because, seriously, he's the most amazing man I could ever have wished to meet.

Wait, I DID wish to meet him. *That's* the point.

What *Is* a Spell?

A spell is simply a prayer in action. It's an active way of manifesting.

A spell can be as simple as sitting somewhere in nature, wishing something and sending your desire out into the universe (or in my case, to SHE). Or it can be more complex, like my Manifest a Man spell, which was worked over a moon cycle and involved a long list of magical ingredients: herbs, incense, essential oils, coloured candles, ribbons, a rhyme or written invocation and the blessing of particular deities.

The complex ones can get a *little* more complicated and involve some preparation. You'll need to choose the appropriate day for the outcome you want (check correspondences on page 155), the ingredients – either intuitively or by their properties – and the tools.

Then, you need to put more preparation into writing your own words for what you want to manifest, and picking clothes in colours that feel appropriate and essential oils that match the properties you need to attract or dispel. Perhaps you can even pull a tarot or oracle card to help guide you.

These sorts of spells usually happen inside a cast circle, with deities and elements/directions called in before the magic flows. And don't forget to thank the deity and spirit that you called in and then close the circle when you're done either, okay?

Creating Magic

You CAN create magic – whether the higher power you use to do it looks like an ancient goddess, the energetic flow of the universe, or simply hard and fast faith in your own journey and experience. YOU have the power to change things up, to manifest and have a major impact on people and their lives.

Just know this: with great power comes great responsibility. (Yes, I'm quoting from Spiderman. Yes, I'm a comic-book geek.) Responsibility to yourself, responsibility to other people, to your community, to animals and to the Earth.

So how, exactly, do you create magic?

From the earliest times, practitioners of magic have used colour, music, rhythm, chants, hand gestures and bodily postures to create their craft.

For me, magic – and circle and spell casting – ritualizes my intention and commitment to create my desires, and to become the mistress of destiny (while surrendering completely to the outcome).

And that's true whether I want to send love and peace to war-torn parts of the world, to write a thought-provoking blog post that will call women to pay attention to their vaginas, or to publish this book. Magic taps into both internal and external forces to help guide my journey to creating what I need.

The good news is that all you actually need to create magic is…

YOU.

You are the most magical tool of all.

It's your intentions and energies that determine the results of any magical work. Many witches never use any other tool besides their own personal energies; and some of the most powerful workings can be done without ever leaving your sofa. It's the focus, concentration, intentions and desires that reside within YOU that are the real 'tools' of the witch.

That said, there are some really cool external tools too. Just saying.

Here are some of my favourites.

Book of Shadows

A Book of Shadows (BOS) – also known as a Grimoire – is a place for a witch to keep her spells, rituals and other secrets.

Modern witches may have theirs as a folder on their laptops; and I'm pretty sure that, given time, someone will create an app so you can do it on your phone.

But what can I say? I like to keep it really old school, so I have journals full of all the spells I've ever cast, with notes about which ones worked and which ones didn't! I also note all the correspondences I used (oils, herbs, coloured candles, what date I did the spell on and where the moon was on that day.)

I do a lot of heart riffing in my BOS too. I'll start by asking a question and asking for guidance. At first, I'll be the one writing the answer; but with practice, SHE/my consciousness takes over, and I'll receive the medicine/insight I've been looking for.

Examples of what could go into your own BOS:

- The Wheel of the Year and the Sabbats.

- The elements and their correspondences (see page 155).

- Spells and rituals that you gather from different places or write yourself. It's helpful to take notes after you cast each spell to see how you feel different and record the changes that the spell brought into your life.

- Herbs, incenses and oils and their properties – especially keeping track of your own experiments with them and how they affect you.

- Crystals and their properties – again, taking notes of how you feel using different crystals, and what effects they have on your life. All this information will come in handy later on when you want to write your own spells!

- Helpful notes on moon phases and how they affect your spell work.

- Colour properties, candle magic, etc.

- Daily appreciation notes are always good for your mind and soul to raise your vibrations and attract more goodness into your life.

- Interesting or creative ideas, sketches, tools you'd like to make or buy, decorations for your altar, ideas for herbs to plant in your garden… Really, anything you come across and would like to keep for inspiration.

- Recipes for potions, herb blends and Sabbat celebration foods. I currently just have my Ostara honey cakes in mine, but I'm totally going to expand that this year!

- A record of your meditations, visualizations and dreams. Both my mum and nanna did this, and the symbolism and insight they received in dreamtime and through visualizations was incredible. I love that I now have access to them!

With spell casting, it's important to keep a clear, focused mind to achieve the best results. That means regular meditation will be helpful, and you might want to take some notes on your meditations if you have any specific feelings or insights.

The same goes for visualization. After casting a spell, vividly and regularly visualizing your goals in a joyful way will improve your chances of success. So that might be worth taking notes on too.

You can decorate your Book of Shadows however you like. It can be any book that takes your fancy – whether you want to start from scratch in a plain notebook or buy a big, old Harry Potter-style spell book – it's totally up to you.

What Else Do You Need?

Actually, as I said earlier in the chapter, you don't NEED any of these things. They're simply a starting point... but they're great to have if you love rituals, spell casting and ceremony like I do.

Athame (pronounced 'a-tham-ay')

Many witches own one or more ritual knives. These are commonly known as 'athames' in witch circles. In the Scottish traditions, the ritual knife is called a 'yag-dirk'. I just call mine my 'witch's knife' though. There's really no need to complicate things.

As with all ritual tools, an athame is a very personal magical item. Many witches actually make their own blades or personalize purchased ones with runes, carvings and other symbols. The aim is to blend the energy of the tool with its owner's magical intentions.

Modern witchcraft books almost always state that an athame is a 'black-handled, double-edged iron blade.' But many practitioners now use athames made from stainless steel, copper, silver and various other metals, or even carved stone. Some witches have family heirlooms, and some never use a blade at all.

What's most important is that the tool you choose suits you personally. I made mine with a wooden handle and a carnelian arrowhead as my blade; and I use it to cast my circles when creating Lady Landscape ceremonies, because carnelian is the stone of the womb.

One thing most witches and Wiccans do agree on is that magical tools should not be used for any purpose other than ritual work. They often leave their blades 'dull' or unsharpened because of this. However, my nanna was a kitchen witch, so when she chopped herbs for magic, she'd use the same knife for that as she used to chop carrots for a stew, or to butter my bread for jam sandwiches.

It made no difference to her, and I can promise that the magic was just as potent.

Broom

The broom or 'besom' is used for cleansing ritual areas, which is why we have the term 'making a clean sweep'. Many witches have a broom (brushy side up) by their front door or on their porch to protect their homes from unwanted outside energies.

You can learn how to make your own besom on page 115.

Cauldron

In contemporary witchcraft, the cauldron is an important magical tool that symbolically combines the influences of the ancient elements of Air, Fire, Water and Earth. Its shape represents Mother Nature, and, as I mentioned earlier, it also represents the cosmic cauldron and the pelvic bowl.

The three legs that a cauldron stands on also correspond to the three aspects of the Triple Goddess (maiden, mother and crone), and to the three lunar phases (waxing, full and waning). In fact, they generally correspond to three as a magical number.

Additionally, the cauldron is a symbol of transformation (both physical and spiritual), enlightenment, wisdom, the womb, the Mother Goddess, and rebirth.

Since early times, cauldrons have been used not only for boiling water and cooking food, but also for heating magical brews, poisons and healing potions. And of course, they've been utilized by alchemists and witches as tools of divination, containers for sacred fires and incense and holy vessels for offerings to the gods of old.

Chalice

The chalice or cup is used to represent the female principle of Water. And, like the cauldron, it's also a representation of our pelvic bowl as the Holy Grail.

Chalices can be made from any material. Many are silver or pewter (be careful with untreated metals when serving wine: you don't want to ruin the chalice OR the wine, right?), but ceramic ones are also quite popular now. Some witches have a selection of different chalices for different types of rituals.

The chalice is sometimes passed around the circle so each person there may take a sip from the same cup. Participants often speak the words: 'May you never thirst!' as they pass the chalice.

They may also pour libations of wine or water from the chalice outside to honour the Old Ones, then offer 'Sabbat' cakes or moon cakes (cakes baked under the energy of, and with ingredients that are supported by, that particular Sabbat and/or moon) back to the Source too.

Clothing

Clothing is optional for many witches. If you're dedicated into a specific tradition, like Gardnerian for example, you may practise 'skyclad'.

If you do wear clothing during your ritual, that clothing – your robe, cape, jewellery and other items – is usually kept just for ritual. Having special garments lends a magical feel and sets ritual work apart from your mundane life.

I have a 'witch wrap' that I only wear for spell working. I also have a necklace that I wear only for ceremonies, and a badass cloak to wear to outdoor rituals. (It's black, with blood-red lining – and it's *hot*.)

Many traditions or paths have a 'standard' wardrobe that reflects the ethnic background of that path. Scots may wear kilts, and Druids may wear hooded robes. Many practitioners embroider magical symbols on their ritual clothing or 'hide' small magical items in the seams and hems to act as talismans for protection.

I have crystals and sigils in the lining of my cloak.

Incense Burner

This is a container that's used to hold a hot coal for burning incense, so it's best made from a fire-resistant or fireproof material.

The most common incense burners are brass and iron 'mini-cauldrons', which come in wonderful shapes and sizes.

The incense itself represents the element of Air, while the smouldering charcoal represents Fire. Together, these two elements are used to purify ritual areas, other tools or the circle itself.

Wand

The wand represents the element of Air and the male East. You can purchase a ready-made wand, or collect one from your friendly neighbourhood tree. (Ask first if you want to harvest one from a living tree; and leave a small token of thanks like a crystal, some incense or a libation of gratitude.)

You can use a wand to cast a circle or direct energy in other magical ways, such as in spells and incantations. There are wands of glass, copper, silver and other metals, but the 'classic' material is still wood (and various woods have different magical associations and uses).

It's very common for a 'wand witch' to have many wands of various types in her magical closet. And other witches who do not use athames often use a wand instead.

Me? I have an athame *and* a wand; but most of the time, I simply use my pointer finger. Trust me: it's just as powerful.

NOTE: use your tools until you don't need them any more. I love my witchy tools, and sometimes I use them, sometimes I don't. Tools don't make you spiritual, and don't make you a witch, but they *can* be a touch point: a connection to your inner wisdom.

Correspondences, Signs and Symbols for Spell Work

Correspondences are lists of all sorts of things – days of the week, colours, numbers, herbs, oils, goddesses and zodiac signs – along with their properties/benefits, and what they can be used in harmony with to attract the same result in magic spells.

So, for example, if I was looking to create a spell for love, I could use a rose quartz crystal, ylang ylang oil and the Lovers tarot card. And I could do the spell on a Friday because it's Goddess Freya's day, and she represents love in the Northern Tradition.

What I share below are just *some* of the correspondences that I work with. They're a Gypsy/Wiccan mashup, and nothing about them is set in stone.

Remember: these are traditions, not dogmas, and the meanings of each correspondence will vary between traditions.

So respect traditions, but follow your feelings. And if in doubt? Leave it out.

Days of the Week

Monday

Ruling Planet: the moon

Colours: white, silver, grey, pearl

Tarot Card: the High Priestess

Herbs and Oils: jasmine, lotus, gardenia, lemon balm

Crystals: carnelian

Powers: divination and female issues

Chakra: root chakra

Best for: emotionally based spell work such as attracting confidence and intuition, protection spells, clairvoyance, astrology, children, divination, dreams/astral travel, household activities, imagination, initiation, magic, new-age pursuits, psychology, reincarnation, religion, short trips, spirituality, the public, totem animals and trip planning.

Tuesday

Ruling Planet: Mars

Colours: red, pink, orange

Tarot Card: the Wheel of Fortune

Herbs and Oils: nutmeg, sage, clove

Crystals: amethyst, lepidolite

Powers: courage, confrontation and strength

Chakra: sacral chakra

Best for: inspiring passion and energy, such as a spell to boost confidence. Mars is a warrior, so if you need a spiritual battle, this is the day for it. Tuesday is also a good day for protection spells, aggression, business, beginnings, combat, confrontation, courage, dynamism, gardening, guns, hunting, movement, muscular activity, passion, partnerships, physical energy, police, repair, sex, soldiers, surgery, tools and woodworking.

Wednesday

Ruling Planet: Mercury

Colours: blue, magenta, silver

Tarot Card: the Magician

Herbs and Oils: peppermint, caraway, fennel, dill, lavender

Crystals: agate, aventurine, lapis lazuli

Powers: travel, money, academic success

Chakra: solar plexus chakra

Best for: communication (worldly or otherwise). Also good for spells involving information-granting, accounting, astrology, communication, computers, correspondence, editing, education, healing, hiring, journalists, learning, languages, legal appointments, messages, music, phone calls, siblings, signing contracts, students, visiting friends, visual arts, wisdom and writing.

Thursday

Ruling Planet: Jupiter

Colours: green, metallic colours

Tarot Card: the Tower

Herbs and Oils: ginger, cumin, frankincense

Crystals: red jasper, garnet, ruby

Powers: jobs, careers, friendships, wealth

Chakra: heart chakra

Best for: probably the best day for spell work generally, as Jupiter is so benevolent and loves to give. All prosperity spells, luck, abundance and success spells should be done on this day (be sure to keep it with the waxing moon). Additionally, spells of business, charity, college, doctors, education, expansion, forecasting, foreign interests, gambling, growth, horses, long-distance travel, luck, material wealth, merchants, philosophy, psychologists, publishing, reading, religion, researching, self-improvement, sports and studying the law.

Friday

Ruling Planet: Venus

Colours: pink, white

Tarot Card: the Lovers and the Empress

Herbs and Oils: mint, rose absolute, ylang ylang

Crystals: rose quartz, rhodonite

Powers: love, sex, relationships

Chakra: throat chakra

Best for: ahhh, sweet love: this is a day for love spells, and is also a good day to offer your love to the gods/goddesses of choice. As the Cure sang, 'It's Friday I'm in Love!' Additionally, it's good for spells of affection, alliances, architects, artists, beauty, chiropractors, courtship, dancers, dating, designers, engineers, entertainers, friendships, gardening, gifts, harmony, luxury, marriage, music, painting, partners, poetry, relationships, romantic love, shopping and social activity.

Saturday

Ruling Planet: Saturn

Colours: black, grey, red, white

Tarot Card: the World

Herbs and Oils: patchouli, comfrey

Crystals: jet, obsidian, onyx

Powers: esoteric/occult knowledge, banishing of limitations, legal issues

Chakra: brow chakra

Best for: banishing spells and ridding old energies. Binding spells are also potent on this day, and it's good for focusing and developing patience (something a lot of witches don't have). Typically, I don't do spells on Saturdays unless it's to get rid of unwanted energies or desires. Other spell work for this day includes justice, karma, limits, obstacles, plumbing, protection, reality, sacrifice, separation, structure, teeth, tests, transformation.

Sunday

Ruling Planet: the Sun

Colours: yellow, gold, orange

Tarot Card: the Sun

Herbs and Oils: sandalwood, rosemary, frankincense

Crystals: amber, sun stone

Powers: growth, healing, male health issues

Chakra: crown chakra

Best for: truth in all matters. The sun is great for truth spells and generating warmth in your heart. If you feel that you're frigid inside and holding tons of resentment, use the sun energy on Sundays to shine through a cloudy heart. Also good for ambition, authority figures, career, children, crops, drama, fun, goals, health, law, personal finances, promotion, selling, speculating, success, volunteers and civic services.

Colours

Using coloured candles to hold the energy/ intention of your wish/ dream/desire while they burn is a great (and inexpensive) way to cast a spell.

Many witches will anoint their candle with oil or herbs too. For example, if you're doing a money spell, you'd choose a green candle and anoint it with ginger and/or frankincense either in herb or oil form.

Get creative with the following colour correspondences:

- **Red**: sex, desire, vitality, strength
- **Orange**: charm, confidence, joy, jealousy, persuasion
- **Yellow**: intellectual development, joy, intellectual strength
- **Green**: prosperity, abundance, fertility, money matters
- **Blue**: healing, protection, spiritual development
- **Purple**: the occult, power, magic
- **Pink**: love, friendship, compassion
- **White**: purity, innocence, peace, tranquillity

The Elements

The elements – Earth, Air, Fire, Water, Spirit/Ether – make us who we are, so I invoke them each and every time I cast a circle.

Depending on the tradition you follow, and where you are in the world, you may call the elements in at different compass points. You might also use each element to represent different things. As I mentioned previously, I've had Wiccan, Strega and Shamanic teachers; and all of them called in the directions and the elements associated with them differently.

If you refer to the opening and closing ceremonies I share in this book, you'll see the way I do it. Feel free to use that yourself, but if it doesn't feel good to you or the land that you stand on, find a different way to acknowledge the elements that does.

Casting a Spell

Casting spells is innately creative.

There's no right or wrong way to create a spell, as long as it works for you. Some witches like a very dramatic setting with ritual and ceremony that can go on for hours. But in general? I'd say give yourself about an hour.

What's important is that you cast your spell with honesty, clarity, focus and intent.

Set an intention

Do you want to bring more abundance into your life?

Let go of something?

Find a healing solution for yourself or a family member?

Mark a life passage or threshold?

Whether it's a spiritual question or a mundane matter, you can bring it into the safe container and meaning-infused space that an intentional circle creates.

Plan what you need

Think about which items will represent your intention for your altar.

Gather offerings for whichever deities or beings are connected to your spell, as well as offerings or candles for each of the four directions and elements. Think of ways to represent your intention in form.

For example, if you want to release something, you could write it down and then burn it. If you want cleansing, you could sprinkle water. You may also want to use chanting or drumming or a rattle to raise the energy once you've created sacred space.

Note: you don't want to have to run out for supplies halfway through a spell, so if you need a certain kind of flower for your altar, water from the sea for a purification spell, or a specific-coloured candle, make sure you know what you need and get it *before* you do the spell.

Then make sure you'll be undisturbed by any interruptions in your sacred space. There's no quicker way to break the energy you create than getting a knock at your door. I always turn my doorbell off if I'm working a spell, too: you can guarantee that the time I go into ritual will be the exact time my parcel is delivered.

Keep in mind that very simple spells and ceremonies can be just as powerful as fancy, all-singing-all-dancing ones. As far as I'm concerned, there's no right or wrong way to do a ceremony. (Although others from much more formal witchcraft traditions will disagree with this, just so you know.)

Make an offering

Before you begin your spell, make an offering to anything – or anyone – that's helped you along the way. Perhaps make an offering to SHE, the spirits, the universe, God/dess, whatever feels comfortable. You can also make an offering to the Earth.

As your offering, you can give a flower, play a singing bowl, sprinkle water or salt, sing a song or shake a rattle.

Cleanse, purify, ground and centre

Many traditions believe that there should always be a period of purification before any ritual. During this period, participants can clear away any worries, concerns and anxieties that may hamper their concentration.

Some traditions burn sage, or sprinkle salt or blessed water (or both). Others burn palo santo or a copal and frankincense mix. And still others use breath work. Choose whichever one feels good for you.

I like to burn sage in the space I'm holding the circle in first, then ask any negative energy to leave so that only loving, supportive energy is left.

If you're sharing space, it's also nice to 'sage' your sisters as they come into circle, starting from their heads, then moving down, front to back. It's a way of blessing them into the space, and marking that they have entered a space of magic, remembrance, sacredness and honour.

Cast a circle

Witches do much of their 'work' in circle. This is where spells are cast, rituals are performed and tools are consecrated

It's also where I practise pretty much anything I consider sacred. I cast a circle whenever I read tarot, before I work with clients and before I do an online or in-person ceremony. I cast one each and every time I sat down to write this book.

By casting the circle, you create sacred space: a 'world between worlds'.

It's a space that not only contains and amplifies the energy you raise in it, but also creates a barrier to deflect any negative energies that may be harmful. It's a place where the creative forces of the universe gather with you to make magic.

The circle is a microcosm of the universe: 'As Above, So Below'. And whatever is created in the circle will eventually manifest in the visible world.

❧ How to Cast a Circle ☙

How you cast a circle is really up to you, but this is how I do it...

Trace out a circle on the ground with a wand, athame, your hand or finger. Keep in mind that whatever tool you use doesn't have to actually *touch* the ground. You simply need to point it down.

Visualize protective energy coming from within you, and direct it down your casting arm (generally your dominant arm). Focus the energy through your casting tool, and visualize a beam of energy coming from it and settling on the ground.

Some practitioners like to cast a circle multiple times (for example, once for protection, once for focus, and once for power); but again, it's not necessary.

Some also like to call the four quarters and elements (East, South, West and North; and Air, Fire, Water and Earth) as they cast, especially if their ritual involves invocations or presence with the Divine.

Additionally, sometimes a circle is marked with candles, stones, cord or some other physical marker. Regardless, it's usually imagined as a sphere or dome of energy.

Keep in mind that the stronger your visualizations are, the better circle you'll cast. Take your time, and focus.

Your ceremony needs a container that's safe and infused with personal and collective meaning.

When we've cast the circle, we begin the ceremony.

Set up your altar

An altar helps to set your focus for rituals, ceremonies and magical workings. In circle, you'd usually place the altar in the North, but this can differ with tradition and geography. This space should be alive and teeming with energy.

I'd suggest not using an altar just for decoration. Instead, make sure the items you place on it are purposeful and have meaning to you, the spell or the ritual. They should be items that provide you with focus and inspiration.

This is your work space, so it should be large enough for you to conduct your spiritual work on. That means you don't want to overwhelm your space with unnecessary statues, knick-knacks and unused objects.

And lastly, your altar should represent your personal beliefs. This is a spiritual altar, and you'll want to honour your beliefs and the divine energies that are present in your space. If you work with specific gods or goddesses, a statue from a pantheon you align with would be good. Alternatively, include a picture or image that symbolizes the deity you wish to call in to oversee your spiritual workings.

What to put on your altar when doing spell work

- **A ceremonial candle**: this is a general-purpose candle used to begin and set the focus of your energy and protection every time you come to sit in front of your altar or do magical working.

- **Ritual candles**: these are candles that you may want to use within your specific ritual or spell work. They can be different colours, depending on the spell and the work they need to do.

- **A set of bowls**: these hold any ingredients that you'll use in your workings. Personally, I have a set of four coloured, ceramic bowls. Each one represents one of the four elements: blue for Water, yellow for Air, green for Earth and red for Fire.

- **A mixing bowl or cauldron**: this is for you to combine your working ingredients in.

- **A ritual cup/chalice**: I share wine or grape juice as part of my workings.

- **Your Grimoire or Book of Shadows**: whether you're referring to your book for information or using it to record your experiences, make a place for it.

Of course there are some traditionalists who believe that an altar should always have specific items in specific locations. While I don't entirely agree, I do think that an altar for magic and spell working needs to be an intentional creation.

I have lots of altars. For example, my body is an altar. I've literally inked my devotion to SHE and my path on my body.

Our house also has an altar in the living room dedicated to the God and Goddess with pictures of heavyweight champion Thor Björnsson and the hugging saint Amma. Plus, every time I write a book, I create an altar specifically for that book and its contents and add talismans, crystals and a tarot pull to support the writing practice.

I also have an altar box dedicated to my menstrual bleed: it's a shoebox containing my favourite chocolate, a ring I wear when I'm bleeding and a picture of the goddess Lilith, who oversees my bleed. I take the box out when I start to bleed; and then when I stop, I put it away again.

> *'Anything you place on the altar is then altered.'*
> — MARIANNE WILLIAMSON

Note: Altars aren't just for spell work. They're also sacred space for communing with spirit, for charging items with spiritual energy, and for you to come to daily to meditate and focus your intent on wishes, dreams and desires.

My friend and witchy sister, Sarah Starrs says: It's important not to get caught up in *what* to put on your altar: this is a spiritual exercise, not a consumer one. In fact, if you're creating an altar for the first time, I'd encourage you to arrange it using only items you already have. You can collect new pieces over time, but you don't want to get stuck thinking that you need something new in order to begin to build your altar.

Remember: an altar is about creating a sacred space for yourself and for your rituals and daily practice, so make *that* your first priority rather than just focusing on the specific things that go on it.

What to put on your everyday altar

Your everyday altar can contain absolutely anything you want, and each item you choose will be personal to you. That said, here are some ideas to get you started:

- **Tarot cards:** pick one for the day, the week or the month, and put it on your altar to remind you of its message.

- **Crystals:** pick ones that carry the energy of whatever you currently want more of in your life.

- **Candles:** I often choose these based on their colour symbolism, or I'll carve words or sigils into them.

- **Statues:** include figurines of any deities you pay tribute to, or whose myths represent qualities you want to embody.

- **Paper:** a written list of your current desires and intentions.

- **Offerings to the gods you honour:** this could be food, flowers, alcohol, spices or anything else that will show them your devotion and gratitude.

- **A plant:** this represents all of the good things you want to have grow in your life. You could even write these things down and tuck them into the soil for added magic.

- **Talismans or pendants**: objects that you want to infuse with the energy of your altar
- **Totems**: objects representing the four elements (a feather, a bowl of water, a vial of dirt and a candle, for example), or others representing your biggest dreams.
- **A vessel of water**: this is said to bring more flow to your life.
- **Coins**: or other symbols of prosperity and abundance.
- **Essentials oils**: for anointing candles and yourself.
- **Your vision board**: or any photographs that evoke your ideal life.

The possibilities are really endless here, but the purpose is to collect items that are beautiful, sacred or meaningful to you.

Writing a Spell

A spell is simply a combination of words that has meaning to you.

You really don't need me to tell you how to write one. You can get as creative as you want, or keep it super-simple.

Just remember: words hold meaning. That's why, when we put them together, we call it 'spelling'. Here are the steps I use to write spells.

Get clear on what you want

What is it that you really want? In 10 days, or in 20 years? What is it *exactly*?

Obviously your desires can change from month to month or year to year. That's why witches work with the phases of the moon – if you change your mind, you can change your goal using the specific phases accordingly.

Write it down

Putting your intentions and dreams onto paper can be a profound experience. Seeing your vision in words offers you the chance to truly visualize it; and in a sense, makes it more real than when it was just in your head.

Additionally, having the words on paper makes you feel accountable for making things happen. So it's possible to increase your own influence over these events just by seeing them written down on paper.

Really try to invoke your vision and experience how great it would make you feel. What are the feelings? Is it the feeling of being safe? Being seen? Is it having the thrill of your creativity reach a wider stage? Don't limit yourself in your thinking.

Believe and take action

You must believe that what you want to transpire will unfold in your life in due time. You must believe it in every fibre of your being. Right down deep into your core.

Then, once you've got *that* down, you have to take action towards the dream/path. If you want to start your own business, buy a URL and sign up for a class on how to use social media effectively. If you want to run a marathon, start running – even if it's just around the block. You need to set the wheels in motion so that both you and SHE/the universe/All That Is know that you mean business.

I never fail to be amazed at how SHE/the universe conspires to help me out when I make a decision, commit to my belief and take action in the service of that desire.

Let it go

Once you've asked for what you want, taken action to start the ball rolling on your desires, and truly believe that what you wish to manifest *will* come true and that you deserve it, you must detach from the outcome completely.

You need to trust that all is right, everything is happening as and when it should; and that your desires will come into fruition in sweet, divine timing. Focus on what you CAN control, in other words: the steps that *you* need to take to keep moving on your path.

Recalibrate and trust

Practical magic is rarely instant. Okay, sometimes it is; but most of the time it, takes feeding, nurturing, work and positivity. That's why it's called spell 'work'.

So recalibrate or tweak if you need to… and most importantly, trust that the magic IS happening.

My motto?

This or something better.

Perform the Spell, Make the Magic

Chant the spell, share the wisdom, stir the cauldron, call in what you need, blow your intentions into a seed and plant them. Pour water on the Earth to symbolize healing for the planet. Write down and burn what you need to clear. Perhaps you feel the need to spontaneously dance or add something during the spell.

I usually have an idea of what I'd like to do in circle, and for the most part, my intention is super-clear. But the rest? I like to really allow SHE to lead me. That way it feels full of meaning to me, in that moment.

Notice who or what shows up during the spell.

Everything is a message. That's what my nanna used to say. Hold symbols and signs with total reverence, even if they come in unexpected ways.

In fact, ESPECIALLY if they come in unexpected ways.

Close the Circle

When you're finished, make sure to close your sacred space. Thank each of the directions and elements that you chose to work with and called in.

Take a moment to pat down your body and arrive fully back into THIS world, before interacting with others or driving a car. I find that putting my hands in soil or on Mumma Nature, eating chocolate or having sex are the best ways for me to ground after ritual.

Ways to Focus Your Intent

Intent is THE thing.

Everything else? Well, it's all frills and fancy spiritual knickers. Don't get me wrong, I LOVE frills and fancy knickers – they're just not essential.

There are so many ways in which we can focus that intent. My favourites are making a mojo bag, creating a sigil – an inscribed or painted symbol considered to have magical powers, and working magic with witches' ladders and bottles. Each of these can be found in many witch and shamanic traditions, but what I share below is how *I* create and work with them.

Mojo Bags

During the dark moon, my nanna used to make small, sewn protection bags containing herbs that she'd whispered magic incantations over. I'd have to wear these and keep them hidden until they fell off, or until the next dark moon (whichever came first).

In Hoodoo, they do something similar and called it a mojo or gris-gris bag.

❧ MAKE A MOJO BAG ☙

You can purchase mojo bags ready-made; but c'mon, you're a creatrix. It's always more powerful to make your own.

What you need to do

Cut two pieces of material in a colour that's specific to your dream/ desire/spell.

Sew three of the sides using thread in a colour that corresponds with your spell too, and leave one edge unsewn to add your contents.

Mojo Bag Contents

Traditional items for mojo bags might have included roots, dirt, herbs and coins.

If you're creating an abundance mojo bag, you could add coins and a piece of ginger, and you can create a sigil specifically for it. If the spell is for you, also add something that represents yourself, even if it's just writing your name on a piece of paper and folding it three times. Just make sure that each item that goes into a mojo bag has a specific purpose, and supports your main intention.

When you've added your contents, breathe your breath into the bag, and either sew it up or tie with a ribbon.

Now tap it three times to wake its magic; and if you're making it at a dark moon, be sure to 'feed' the bag (add a few drops of an oil that corresponds with the magic of the bag), then wear it.

But remember, you have to keep it hidden for the magic to work!

⌒⊙⌒

Power sigils

A power sigil can help you to realize and manifest a dream or desire into being.

To make it, you can use a coloured ink that's specific to your desire (refer to the colours for candle magic on page 160). Or, once you've created it, you might want to sew it onto a piece of clothing using the thread of the associated colour.

⌒ CREATE A POWER SIGIL ⌒

Write your wish on paper using coloured ink.

Go through the words of your desire/wish and cross out any repeating letters. So, for example, If your wish is 'I need a new house', you'd be left with I, n, e, d, a, w, h, o, u and s.

Now it's time to get creative. Draw a circle, and within it, find a way to combine the curves and lines of each letter to create your own sigil specific to this desire.

When I create these sigils, I put a copy in my purse, another on my wall and sometimes I even ink it on my skin in pen. Some practitioners suggest folding the paper you write it on four times and placing that in the ground, while others suggest drawing the sigil in Dragon's Blood ink and imbuing it with a corresponding essential oil.

If you're also making a mojo bag, add your sigil to that.

❦

Witches' ladder

A witches' ladder is like a rosary for witches; except instead of passing the rosary through your fingers and repeating an incantation, you whisper, sing or chant your spell as you create and braid the ladder with your hands.

How to Make a Witches' Ladder

To cast a spell with a witches' ladder, take three pieces of string, ribbon or yarn – preferably in colours relevant to your intent (to check out correspondences, go to page 155).

To cast the spell, focus your intent on the ribbons; and as you braid them, 'weave your desire' into the braid by singing, whispering or chanting it. As you plait, you can also add little tokens: feathers, charms, shells, beads and any other objects that feel right to you and align with whatever you're creating the charm for. You can weave in as few as nine of these tokens or as many as 40: it's entirely up to you.

Once you're finished, use the charm to draw your desire by hanging it somewhere in your home, burying it on your property or using it for meditation.

❦

I still have the very first ladder I made (with kitchen witch, friend and fellow author Rachel Patterson) hanging in my office. We made our ladders sitting at her kitchen table; and mine has a specific protection and creativity spell imbued into it. I rub it often; and sometimes, when I sit in meditation, I'll chant with it to renew its energy.

Remember that shop-bought witches' ladders are good for meditation – and you can obviously enchant them (cleanse and infuse them with your intent and power) if you want – but they'll never give you the power of a home-made ladder.

When you create something with your own hands, you completely infuse it with your energy.

A witches' bottle

Spell bottles, also known as 'witches' bottles', have been in use in England and the United States since at least the 1600s.

They were originally created to destroy the power of an evil magician or witch thought to have cast a spell against the bottle's creator, and were often ceramic vessels, filled with hair, nails and even the victim's urine. They were also built into the walls of new homes as magical guardians. Spell bottles of this type continued to be used well into the 19th century.

You can make spell bottles or jars (I use jam jars when I make mine) for a variety of purposes, and use them in numerous ways. Some are buried or otherwise hidden, while others are placed in windows of the home or in other prominent spots. All are concentrations of energy, created and empowered for specific magical purposes.

Witches' bottles are a very powerful way to protect your space. You can make one and bury it on your property (if you live in an apartment or a flat, you might want to bury it in a potted plant that you keep at your door) to attract any negativity and stop it from entering your home. Or you can make a witches' bottle to attract prosperity or good luck. I have one in the wealth corner of my home, which is sealed with green candle wax and infused with herbs to attract abundance. It's really simple, but super-effective.

◌❧ WITCHES' BOTTLE ❧◌
ᶠOR PROTECTION

Gather rosemary, needles, pins and red wine. Fill a small jar with the first three, saying while you work:

Pins, needles, rosemary, wine; in this witches' bottle of mine. Guard against harm and hostility; this is my will, so mote it be!

Visualize the bottle or jam jar doing just that as you continue to fill it.

When the jar is full, pour in the red wine. Then cap or cork the jar, and drip wax from a red or black candle to seal it. Bury it at the farthest corner of your property or put it in a discreet spot in your house.

Draw a banishing pentagram in the dirt above it. This destroys negativity and evil: the pins and needles impale evil, the wine drowns it and the rosemary sends it away from your property.

∽ MONEY SPELL BOTTLE ⌣

Place old pennies, dried corn, seeds, rice, cinnamon sticks, cloves and whole allspice into a bottle or jar until it's filled to the top. Cap it tightly.

Shake the bottle with your dominant hand for five minutes while chanting these or similar words:

'Herbs and silver, copper and grain; Work to increase my financial gain.'

Place the money spell bottle on a table somewhere in your house. Leave your purse, pocketbook, wallet and/or chequebook near the bottle when you're at home. Allow money to come into your life.

∽⌣

Women are source.

So of *course* we create.

Life, spells, family, magic, art, business, money and love. We create it ALL. We create from our bodies, our will, our minds and our feelings.

We create them ourselves, with Mumma Nature, sister witches, family and lovers.

But most of all, we create from ourselves.

We are source.

You are source.

You are a Creatrix.

I am a Creatrix.

The 'Wake the Witch' Project

Ways to Invoke SHE Who Dreams, Manifests and Makes Magic:

Manifesting Maven: be intentional but don't fixate on the end result.

Know what it is you desire, set clear intentions and focus your energy in that direction. Then let go of all expectations as to how it will manifest.

You'll find that SHE/the universe/Goddess/All That Is will deliver, just rarely in the way you'd planned it.

Altar-rations: create sacred space. Your altar doesn't have to be big: some of my most favourite altars have been shoeboxes that I've had to put away after use because I was living in a small locale.

Use it as a space to pay reverence daily, or set it up for a moon cycle to support you in creating and completing a spell or work project.

Express Yourself: creation and creativity come in many different forms – from casting spells to making a baby to moving your body to starting a revolution based on something you feel strongly about.

However SHE moves through you, allow yourself to express it fully.

Share it ALL from THAT place.

Chapter 10

The Oracle

*SHE Who Trusts Her Intuition
and Sees All Things*

Her intuition was her
favourite super-power.

*'To practise magic is to bear the
responsibility for having a vision.'*

— STARHAWK

Being a witch is a path of learning. There might be moments when you think, *Yes, I've TOTALLY got this whole life thing figured out.* Then, in the next heartbeat, you'll find yourself in the void – the cosmic womb – smack-dab in the centre of the mystery of it all, and knowing absolutely bloody NOTHING.

THIS is the path of the witch.

Some of it you'll get from reading books. But honestly?

Most of it will be experiential, and you'll 'feel' it. You can read *all* the books about setting up an altar, reading tarot, trusting your instinct and casting spells. But until you've experienced a truth for yourself – until you've seen an actual dream you've had come true – you won't truly have the knowing.

The more you practise, the more you'll begin to trust yourself, and the more you'll begin to trust THAT knowing.

When you talk about the witch, what you're really talking about is the mystery.

Some believe that certain information will be passed down to them as they progress in their learning and practice. And this can be true, but not in the way that most of us think.

The simple fact is that no one can teach or tell you 'the mysteries'. They're the 'aha' moments and realizations that unfurl and reveal themselves as a result of your own spiritual experiences and your menstrual cycle, and through circle work, self-sourcing and direct contact with Mumma Nature.

You may find, like I did writing this book, that when you try to share your knowledge, you have trouble putting it into words. It's not because you can't write or speak, but because the realizations you experience when you try to share are so profound that they sound too simple and unimpressive when you try to express them.

Yes, you can definitely develop your intuitive powers through visualization, dream work and circle work. But developing your *witch* powers is not so much about predicting lottery numbers or knowing which tarot card means what.

Instead, it's about enhancing your sensitivity and response towards both random thoughts and direct, loaded truth bombs. It's knowing what's for you and what's for other people, and learning how to make sense of emotional changes within your body.

It may even be as simple as having a sense of when the phone is going to ring or knowing whether that tummy ache you're experiencing is something you ate for dinner or a red flag that something isn't right.

> **This is about building a relationship of total love, appreciation and trust with yourself, your body and your psyche.**

And one of the witch's greatest powers – one that the books don't teach you – is patience.

This reconnection with the Self and remembrance of your magic takes time, dedication, and lifelong commitment to the incredible, awesome, complicated and delicious messiness that is you.

She Who Remembers

When I went to Mnajdra – a 5,000+ year-old temple in Malta – for the first time, I remembered. This ancient temple dedicated to the

Goddess is one of many on this little Mediterranean island; but this particular one on the west coast, looking out to sea, has been home for me.

I know it.

They say 'once a witch, always a witch'; and standing barefoot in that temple, I remembered.

I remembered that the onset of Patriarchy didn't kill the Goddess. She simply lay dormant underground in the darkness, growing roots. Really strong bloody roots, because she's cyclic; and she knew that with every Great Forgetting, where women and their power are put in the dark, there had to come a Great Remembering.

That Great Remembering is now.

And we need the Oracles to show us the way.

In the Maltese Goddess temples, there are designated spaces specifically for the Oracle: a healer who gave predictions and counsel to her community.

So when I saw, and more importantly, *felt* the Oracle's space in the temple of Mnajdra, I knew that if I had to take on any specific 'witch' label, mine would be 'Oracle'.

What Is an Oracle?

Called on to provide wise and insightful counsel and/or prophetic predictions of the future inspired by the gods, an Oracle offers answers to life's questions and mysteries. Sometimes she may pull a tarot card, sometimes she'll enter a trance-like state and communicate with other beings and worlds. But mostly, in my experience, a modern-day Oracle shares the very best counsel when she remembers herself – the deep intuitive trust of the wisdom and knowing held in her body.

An Oracle remembers herself
and her innate
Goddess-given powers.

When Socrates asked how he could become wiser, the Oracle of Delphi told him: 'Know Thyself.' That advice wasn't just for Socrates, it was for us all. Of course we can, and will continue to, look to teachers and guides – not so that they can tell us what to 'do', but so they can be a mirror to our own remembrance of what we already know.

That woman is an Oracle.

She connects with nature and her cycles. She knows how to give healing and apply it, first and foremost to herself, before then sharing it with others.

She hears – and more importantly – pays attention to the voice of her womb. And is naturally led to show up and help others to remember, reconnect and reclaim the wisdom of their wombs, too.

She connects and communicates with other worlds, life forms and dimensions, and shares and decodes the messages, symbols, sounds and signs that she discovers there.

She tells stories and creates art. She collects poems and songs. She remembers stories that have been forgotten. (Or burned, or silenced or HEAVILY edited to suit the needs of another. Yes, Patriarchy, I'm talking to you.)

Any time we fully trust ourselves – our body, our wisdom, our gut instinct, our knowing – we become an Oracle.

Divination

To be able to trust your intuition, yourself and the Divine, developing and practising divination skills WILL help.

Fortune telling is probably the oracle craft most closely associated with the Gypsy people. My nanna, always one to keep it simple, said it was 'Finding out about the future, before it happens.'

You can learn about the future through various oracular methods. Personally, I use tarot cards, shamanic journeying with a drum, dreamtime and water scrying.

These tools offer me ongoing guidance about which paths to take, and which to avoid. But that's not the real value of this practice. 'Telling fortunes' is merely a side effect – and not a very important one when you consider the real potential of it, which is direct communication with divine guidance.

The root of the word divination is, of course, 'divine'.

(No, it's not 'demon' as some religious paths and traditions will have you believe. Just saying.)

Basically, I use these oracular methods to hear the guidance of SHE. The Goddess. The Divine. Sometimes this guidance comes as insight into a problem. Other times it comes as information I needed, or suggestions on what action to take.

Divining is like spending time chatting over tea with your BFF and wisest mentor. Not only are you continually feeding the relationship so it remains strong and healthy, but you're also gaining invaluable advice on everything you need to know in life.

What follows are some of my favourite divining tools and practices. Once again though, they're simply tools. All you ever *really* need when connecting with the Divine is you.

Tarot

To people unfamiliar with divination, it may seem that someone who reads tarot cards is 'predicting the future'.

Not true.

Most tarot card readers will tell you that the cards offer a guideline, which the reader simply interprets as a possible outcome based upon the forces at work.

Anyone can learn to read tarot cards, but it does take some practice. It's a highly intuitive process, so while books and charts will come in handy? The best way to learn what your cards actually mean is to handle them, hold them, sleep with them under your pillow and journey with each one. *Feel* what they're telling you.

I once spent 78 weeks studying a tarot card each week: letting it guide me for that week; studying its messages, signs and symbols; and charting what came up for me. I totally recommend that as a practice.

Tarot decks

There are hundreds of different tarot decks available. Some are based upon famous artwork, books, legends, mythologies and even movies. Choose a deck that feels right for you.

My go-to deck is the Crowley Thoth deck, because the cards in it are so loaded with symbolism. I also have a big love for the Gustav Klimt tarot: the artwork is insanely good.

If you're a new tarot reader who's not sure which deck is best for you, pick up the Rider Waite deck. It's the one that's most often used in the illustrations of tarot instruction books, and it's a fairly easy system to learn.

You can always add new decks to your collection later on. I do, on a near weekly basis. Yes, I *am* obsessed.

About the cards

A tarot deck consists of 78 cards. The first 22 cards are the Major Arcana, which each have symbolic meanings focused on the material world, the intuitive mind and the realm of change.

The remaining 56 cards are the Minor Arcana, which are divided into four groups or suits: Swords, Pentacles (or Coins), Wands and Cups. Each of the four suits also focuses on a theme:

- **Swords**: conflict, mind or moral issues
- **Cups**: emotions and relationships
- **Coins**: material aspects of life, such as security and finance
- **Wands**: jobs, ambition and activity

How do tarot cards work?

Any experienced tarot reader will agree that reading cards is an intuitive process. Like any other form of divination, the cards become a focal point for your own intuition.

You can use any number of different spreads (layouts) in a tarot reading. Some readers use elaborate layouts, while others may just pull out three to five cards and see what they need to see.

One of the most popular layouts is the Celtic Cross. Other well-known spreads include the Tree of Life layout, the Romany spread and the Pentagram Spread (you can find more details of these spreads over at www.wakethewitches.com). You can also do a simple spread, by laying out three, five or even seven cards in any shape you choose for interpretation.

Reversed cards

Sometimes, a card comes up backwards or upside down. Some tarot readers interpret these reversed cards in a way that is the opposite of the card's right-side-up meaning. Other readers may not bother with a reversed interpretation, feeling that the messages may be incomplete.

The choice is yours.

Keep things positive (but keep them real)

Although you may pull half a dozen cards for someone that indicate that all kinds of gloom, doom and destruction are headed their way, try to keep things positive.

If you believe some sort of illness is coming, or that someone's marriage is in trouble, DON'T say, 'Wow, this is bad!' Don't hold back on information, but remind them that things can change at any time, based upon the decisions they choose to make from here.

Read for anyone and everyone who'll let you – and don't be afraid to tell people what you see. Cast a circle before reading if that feels good, call in and connect with the Divine and ask for Her guidance. Then breathe deeply.

Ask the person you're reading for to give you feedback; and eventually, over time, you'll get comfortable with reading the tarot. You'll also begin to trust that what's coming through is information for the person you're reading for, and that you're not just 'making it up'.

Reading the Tea Leaves

One of the most iconic forms of divination is reading tea leaves, also called *tasseography* or *tasseomancy*.

This divination method isn't as ancient as some of the other popular and well-known systems. In fact, in her book *The Encyclopedia of Witches, Witchcraft and Wicca*, Rosemary Guiley points out that during the medieval period, European fortune-tellers often did readings based upon spatters of lead or wax.

When the tea trade boomed, however, these other materials were replaced with tea leaves for 'divinatory purposes'.

Some people use cups that are specially designed for reading tea leaves. These often have patterns or symbols outlined around the rim, or even on the saucer, for easier interpretation. A few sets have zodiac symbols on them too.

But again, you don't need anything fancy. Not really. Just a cup, a connection with the Divine and an open heart. (And tea leaves, obviously.)

How do you read tea leaves?

You'll need a cup of tea made with loose-leaf tea to start with. Make sure you don't use a strainer, because that will eliminate the leaves from your cup. Also ensure you use a white or light-coloured teacup, so you can actually see what the leaves are doing.

After you've drunk the tea, and all that's left in the bottom are the leaves, place the base of the cup in your dominant hand, and swirl the cup in a clockwise direction three times so the leaves settle into a pattern.

Once you've done this, look at the leaves and see if they present you with images. This is where the divination begins.

There are two typical methods of interpreting the images:

- **Learn some of the universal standard symbol interpretations.** For instance, a blob that looks like a dog typically represents a loyal friend. An apple usually symbolizes knowledge or education. There are a number of books available on tea-leaf symbols; and although interpretations vary, the symbols usually have similar meanings.

- **Use your intuition.** This is my preferred choice, and much as with other divination methods, intuitively reading tea leaves is about what the images make you think and feel. That blob of leaves may look like a dog, but what if it doesn't represent a loyal friend at all? What if you're positive it's a warning that someone needs protection? If you're reading intuitively, you'll need to decide whether to trust your instinct or not.

Often, you'll see multiple images. Rather than just seeing that dog right there in the centre, you might also see smaller images around the rim.

In this case, start reading the images in order, beginning with the handle of the teacup and working your way around clockwise. If your cup has no handle, begin at the 12:00 point (the very top, away from you), and go around it clockwise.

Pay particular attention to:

- **What you saw first:** often, the first thing you see in a tea-leaf reading is the most influential thing or person.

- **Letters or numbers:** does that letter 'M' mean something to you? Is it in reference to your sister Mandy, your co-worker Mike or that job you've been looking at in Montana? Trust your instincts.

- **Animal shapes:** animals have all kinds of symbolism – dogs are loyal, cats are sneaky and butterflies represent transformation.

- **Celestial symbols:** do you see a sun, a star or a moon? Each of these has its own meaning. For instance, the moon symbolizes intuition and wisdom.

- **Other recognizable symbols:** do you see a cross? A peace sign? Perhaps a shamrock? Again, each of these has its own meaning, many of which are culturally assigned. Ask yourself what that symbol means to you personally.

Finally, it's worth noting that many tea-leaf readers divide their cup into sections; and where an image appears in the cup is nearly as important as the image itself.

If you divide your cup into three sections, the rim is typically associated with things that are happening right now. If you see an image near the rim, it relates to something immediate.

The centre of the cup, around the middle, is usually associated with the near future (and, depending on who you ask, the near future can be anywhere from a week to a full moon phase of 28 days).

Finally, the bottom of the cup holds the answer, as a whole, to your question or situation as it stands now.

Pendulums

A pendulum is one of the simplest and easiest forms of divination. It's a simple matter of asking a Yes/No question, and having it answered.

A pendulum is usually a pointed crystal on a metal chain. When you first get or make a pendulum, you'll need to calibrate it to figure out how it's going to tell you the answers to your questions.

⤳ CALIBRATE YOUR PENDULUM ⤲

To calibrate your pendulum, simply hold it by the free end of the chain so that the weighted end is loose. Make sure you keep it perfectly still.

Ask a simple Yes/No question to which you already know the answer. For example, I might ask, 'Am I female?' or 'Do I live in the UK?'

As you ask, keep your eye on the pendulum; and when it starts moving, note whether it goes side to side, forwards to backwards, or some other direction. This movement indicates your 'Yes' direction.

Now, repeat the process, asking a question to which you know the answer is No. The movement you get in response will give you your 'No' direction.

It's a good idea to do this a few times with different questions, so you can get a feel for how your pendulum responds specifically to you. Some will swing horizontally or vertically, while others swing in small or large circles. And others don't do a whole lot unless the answer is really important.

Once you've calibrated your pendulum and you've got to know it, you can use it for some basic divination.

Using your pendulum for divination

There are several different ways you can use a pendulum for divination – you'd be surprised what you can learn with 'yes' and 'no' answers. The trick is to learn to ask the right questions. Here are a few options:

- **Use it with a divination board**: some people like to use their pendulum with a board – the pendulum guides them to the letters on the board that spell out a message.

- **Find lost items**: much like a dowsing rod, a pendulum can be used to point in the direction of missing things.

- **Receive answers to more complex questions**: if you have a specific but complex question, try laying out a group of tarot cards with possible answers. Use the pendulum to lead you to the card that has the right answer.

- **Locating magical sites**: if you're outdoors, carry your pendulum with you. Some people believe that ley lines can be located via pendulum use. Oh, and if you happen to stumble across a location that makes your pendulum go crazy, consider holding a ritual or connecting with the Divine there.

Scrying

Scrying is my most favourite witch tool. (Wait, I've said that about everything I've shared so far, haven't I?!)

The word 'scrying' comes from the Anglo Saxon 'descry' which means 'reveal'. The ancient Romans scried in their religious rituals, and the Egyptian Book of The Dead contains references to Hathor's magic mirror, which was used to see the future.

Pre-Christian Celtic seers were also believed to have visions when they looked upon dark stones such as beryl or other crystals, according to Pliny. Even in the 1500s, Nostradamus made notes about staring into a bowl of water by candlelight to gain inspiration.

In occult literature, the term scrying is used to describe the act of gazing at a shiny stone or mirror or into a crystal ball (anything that reflects will do) to see things past and future. When a crystal is used, scrying is known as *crystallomancy*. Some practitioners also use the flame of a candle to scry, which is called *tratakam* in Sanskrit.

If you concentrate hard enough while gazing on any of these objects, you can conjure up visions, because scrying clears out your conscious mind, and opens a direct line to the Divine.

The first step is to pick a scrying tool. You can use anything – from the simplest clear glass filled with water to a crystal sphere, or many variations in between. You could try a mirror, a candle or a piece of black-painted glass. I have a black obsidian scrying bowl, but use whatever feels right for you.

✎ How to Scry ✎

First, prepare the room: cast your circle, dim the lights, burn incense and do whatever makes you feel comfortable.

Put whatever you're using to scry with on a table at a convenient level, and relax with some deep, into-the-womb breaths.

Look at your scrying object in a relaxed manner, focusing just past its surface (or past the flame in the case of a candle).

Don't be too concerned if you need to blink.

Otherwise, just try to keep your mind blank, with the exception of the one question you may wish to ask.

Don't push yourself past 20 minutes the first few times you practise this.

~~

Keep in mind that images appear differently for each person. They may just appear instantly, or they may first appear as a fog that morphs into a clear image. Or sometimes, they'll appear simply as symbols of events: past, present or future.

Practice makes perfect. If you don't succeed at first, keep on trying. Experiment with different techniques and objects to find what works best for you. Everyone is different, and what works for one won't necessarily work for all.

∞ SCRYING BY THE MOON ∞

The ancients also used the full moon to illuminate their scrying tools and provide a reflective surface for their intuitions to work with. Candlelight is also an effective way to illuminate your scrying tool.

If you can't perform this ritual on the night of the full moon, the night immediately before or after is still potent with full moon goodness.

In addition to a clear sky and a full moon, you'll need the following items:

A table or some sort of flat work space (some people scry at their altars too)

A dark bowl: black obsidian scrying bowls are *so* good for this, but you could paint a glass bowl with waterproof black paint too

A jug containing enough water to fill the bowl

A journal and pen

what to do:

If you feel called, cast a circle.

When it's complete, sit or stand comfortably at your work space or altar.

Begin by closing your eyes, and attuning your mind to the energy around you. Feel Mumma Earth under your feet. Hear the wind in the trees.

Breathe in the scents that surround you.

Raise your arms out to your sides, palms facing up, and feel the energy of the moon above you.

Take some time to gather that full moon juju.

When you're ready to begin scrying, open your eyes.

Raise your jug of water to the moon, and ask for it to be charged by her lunar love, before using it to fill the bowl. As you do, visualize wisdom and guidance flowing into the water. Know deep down in your heart and womb that this water can and will show you the mysteries of the moon.

When the bowl is full, position yourself so that you can see the moon's light reflected directly into the water.

Stare into the water, looking for patterns, symbols or pictures. Thoughts may come into your heart and mind that don't seem relevant, but write *everything* down.

When you're finished gazing into the water, make sure you've recorded everything you saw, thought and felt during your scrying session. If a bit of information doesn't make sense, don't worry – sit on it for a few days and let your unconscious mind process it. Chances are that it will make sense eventually.

Afterwards, you can leave your water out overnight to be charged in the moonlight, and then drink it the next morning for a boost of lunar goodness. Or you can pour it onto your garden or a pot plant as an offering.

The Dreamer

On my altar is a stature of the Maltese Dreamer. She's a super-curvy, bountiful woman who, at first glance, looks like she's lying down sleeping. But this little statue is a replica of the one found in the Hypogeum: an underground, labyrinth-like structure that was viewed by those who built her as the womb of the Goddess.

That structure was a dream incubator: a place you came for comfort, healing and divine guidance through dreams. Pregnant women would come and sleep in that chamber so that spirit would come into their foetus. Women *literally* dreamed life into being within a womb.

That's pretty freakin' magical, right?

The song *Returning* by Jennifer Berezan, one that I play on every retreat and in every womb healing session, was recorded there. That song creates an anchor for all women when we listen to it – it helps us to return home to our womb space, because it's *here* in the place of radical rest, that we dream life into being.

Our lives are currently so fast-paced that we rarely have time to dream. Yet it's in our dreaming that we're able to manifest and create.

The ancients knew it.

I know it.

I've sat in the womb tomb at the Hypogeum and asked SHE to show me how it was used. She answered by showing me a vision of the statue of the Maltese Dreamer, bleeding between her legs.

I understood this to mean that the ancients had their very own built-into-their-bodies method of radical rest: menstruation. Yep, back in the day when bleeding with each moon *wasn't* considered a curse, our menstrual bleed was a time to dream. When we shed our blood, we were given our deepest visions, and became natural seers and oracles.

This is yet another of the powers that have been taken from us with the onset of fast-paced, straight-line, goal-oriented, must-do-the-next-thing living.

We feel guilty for not keeping up with men, so we keep working and never resting. We ignore the cycles of the seasons, and the rhythms of our own body. Yet it's in our rest time, specifically when we bleed each month, that we're most open to receive direct communication with SHE, the Divine.

That's why women used to gather in red tents, so that they could be in solitude and receive guidance. It's why womb temples were set up specifically for women to dream and receive visions in. It's why so many women suffer from pain during their bleed: because they're not resting, they're no longer open to receive their SHE-led wisdom.

The pain is a reminder. It's our call to come home to ourselves, to rest and allow ourselves to receive fully. But instead, in order to keep going, many of us simply medicate our bleed, which means we miss out on all the lady magic. The *good* stuff.

(If you no longer bleed, this time of deep rest, connection with the Divine and receiving is still available during the dark of the moon.)

A witch who is woken in the womb
can dream her life into being.

So yes, you *can* scry and read tarot and tea leaves, and you *can* and absolutely *should* cultivate your connection to the moon and Mumma Earth. But if you do nothing except honour your womb as the source of your bloody magic (pun totally intended) and the intuitive centre of your Self, you'll do just fine.

Your womb is an oracle.

You are an Oracle.

I am an Oracle.

The 'Wake the Witch' Project

Ways to Invoke SHE Who Trusts Her Intuition and Sees All Things:

Know thyself: when you know yourself (and this is a lifelong project BTW), trusting your body wisdom with its signs, power points and hotspots, and trusting your ability to 'see into the future', is no longer something that others do. Instead, it's something you know and trust to be true about you. Yes, YOU.

Take responsibility for your decisions and choices: the next time you're faced with a problem or decision, remember that there's no such thing as a 'one right answer' that you have to find. Instead, there's just *your* right answer.

Choose a divination method, connect with your womb or simply close your eyes. Take a few deep breaths. Ask yourself what you'd do if you DID know?

Because you do. You always know.

Rest. Often. If you bleed, the entire second half of your cycle – pre-menstruation and menstruation – is a call to slow down and receive. If you no longer bleed, use the energy of the waning and the dark moon as your guide to help you hone your oracle and divination skills through rest, dreamtime and visionary downloads.

Chapter 11

The Healer

*SHE Who Heals Herself
and Heals the World*

A woman armed with
ancestral wisdom is an
unstoppable force.

It's ALL medicine.

Since the beginning of time, women healers honoured and observed the sacred cycles of nature, time and spirit. They served their communities through midwifery and spiritual, nutritional, hands-on and herbal healing, as well as massage, prayer, ritual, dance, song, music, toning and dreaming.

And they were honoured and revered for their sacred feminine healing arts.

However, in the times of persecution that I spoke about in Chapter 4, patriarchal belief structures targeted women – healers and midwives specifically – and called them all witches. The result was our society experiencing what I can only describe as a 'healer holocaust'.

That's why there's still a fear attached to the word 'healer'. The fear exists, even though many of us can feel the call to heal by working with herbs and oils, making tinctures and teas, and practising healing modalities such as reiki, acupuncture, aromatherapy and the many hundreds in between.

It exists even though some of us feel drawn to explore and experience the teachings of plants like rapé, ayahuasca, iboga and San Pedro; and to serve ourselves and each other through natural healing practices like self-touch, massage and song and dance to heal and nurture.

The fear exists because, for many of us, healing wisdom hasn't been passed down via the elders in our family or community. Instead, we've had to seek the 'how to' from third parties. (FYI: What you think you're being taught? You're actually remembering.)

The fear exists because we live in a world where big pharmaceutical companies promise quick fixes from pills they make in a laboratory. They sanitize healing, put it in clean, sterile packaging, and then call it medicine.

The fear exists because we've been taught that, as women, our intuitive nature is not trustworthy. That WE are not trustworthy.

> *'Woman is by nature a witch, healer,*
> *shaman and medicine healer.'*
> - CHUKCHEE PROVERB

In The Hispanic Curandera, the Polish babka, the Mayan G-mamma, the Appalachian granny midwife; in traditional cultures around the globe, female healers were – and still are – an integral part of a community. Known as the wise woman, herbalist, midwife, village healer or shamana, she would blend her knowledge of herbs, menstruation, illness and midwifery with cultural and esoteric beliefs. She would learn her healing craft from the elder women in her community – often a mother, grandmother, aunt or neighbour – and she would begin a lifelong relationship with the healing arts. A relationship based on her deep connection to nature, a total reverence for the human body and her innate trust of her own knowing. High fives to THAT.

Yep, healing is an art and women's creativity starts in the womb. Not only is it able to birth new human life, it's in this place that women dream, vision and create revelations AND revolutions. Again, more high fives please.

We are co-creators of our life, our reality and the universe. As women, we can heal FAR more than just ourselves and our communities. See? Didn't I tell you we were powerful?

We also have the capacity to midwife the birth of a new way of being here on Earth. I want to keep this as real as I can, but when we remember our power to heal, we can change up our role on this planet. I believe that trying to 'fight' Patriarchy is NOT the answer. Reacting to, and trying to change, what's 'already so' will serve no one. However, YOU connecting to the truth that lies between your thighs? YOU creating a new version of what actually is? YOU remembering how to heal and then using what you remember to heal yourself? Witch, that is a fucking mind-blowing, heart-opening paradigm shifter.

You are the midwife
of the Witch Waking Up.

Now, you could read ALL the books for the next 20 years, never coming up for air, and still only know the very smallest amount of what there is to know about women as healers. I've recommended some of my favourite books in the Wake the Witch Bookshelf section at the back of this book; but for me, it all starts and ends with the breath.

Breath

Breath is the very best kind of medicine.

Breathing, or *pranayama* as it's called in Sanskrit, offers many healing benefits (besides keeping you alive, obvs). Your breath can loosen up muscle tension, release anxiety and allow you to create space in your body and mind.

It's actually quite difficult to breathe properly. We've all got so much to do that few of us pay any attention to the depth of our breath, or that we're even breathing at all.

I love that in yoga, the whole practice of pranayama is dedicated to it: to inhaling and exhaling. When you breathe with awareness, your *whole* body knows about it.

I start every SHE Flow Yoga class I teach with Womb Breaths, because when you breathe directly into your medicine bowl (aka your cauldron, aka your pelvic bowl), you send vital healing energy to your uterus, ovaries, bladder and cervix. You wake them up. You show them love.

In fact, I have a toolbox of breathing techniques that help me to come into a place of complete love and healing in my body.

Healing starts here.

⚮ Breath as Medicine ⚮

Womb and Belly Breath

Place one hand on your lower belly and relax your tummy muscles. Then slowly inhale through your nose, bringing air right down into the bottom of your lungs.

You should feel your tummy rise, which expands the lower parts of your lungs.

Continue to inhale as your ribcage expands outwards; and finally, your collarbones rise. At the peak of your inhalation, pause for a moment and feel your womb space and your tummy filled with love.

Then exhale gently from your womb, past your gut, and out through your mouth as audibly as feels good. Don't be afraid to make noise.

Repeat as many times as feels good.

Ocean Breath (aka Darth Vader Breath)

When you feel angry, irritated or frustrated, try a cooling Ocean Breath, or Ujjayi (pronounced *oo-jai*). This will soothe and settle your mind. Why? Because your breath sounds a lot like the lapping of the ocean on a shoreline. Or Darth Vader.

- Inhale more deeply than in a normal breath. With your mouth closed, exhale through your nose while constricting your throat muscles. If you're doing this correctly, you should sound like waves on the ocean. Or, like I said, Darth Vader.

- Another way to get the hang of this practice is to try exhaling the sound "haaaaah" with your mouth open. Now make a similar sound with your mouth closed, feeling the outflow of air through your nasal passages. See? Darth Vader, right?

- Once you've mastered this on your outflow, use the same method for your inflow breath – again, gently constricting your throat as you inhale.

  Ideally, your breath will sound like the ocean, and you'll visualize Hawaiian beach fronts, warm sand and the sun on your skin. Or you'll just keep thinking you're Darth Vader. Either's good.

⚮

Herbs

Every herb and root has both a medicinal *and* a magical property of some sort. Each one shows its properties and qualities by its form, shape and spirit. And one of the best parts about being an 'awake witch' is that you make it your witch work to learn to hear, see, smell and feel these qualities to understand the gifts from Mumma Earth that are all around us.

Herbs are used in teas and tinctures, to anoint candles, to add power and intention to spell casting, to make incense and to heal ailments. However, the herbs used in witchcraft aren't always the same as the ones used in Conjure and Hoodoo.

Conjure workers tend to use the roots of plants, while witches most often use the leaves and flowers. For this reason, Hoodoo plant lore and practice is called 'rootworking', and witchcraft plant lore and practice is called 'herb magic'.

There are no hard and fast rules though, and there's much overlap between the two traditions. After all, they've influenced each other a lot over the years.

A Few Essentials

It's a good idea to have a basic supply of a few commonly used herbs in your witch's cupboard. If you're doing a spell from a book, it will often have a lengthy list of ingredients. And, especially if the book is not written in your country of origin, some of these may be very hard to come by.

From experience, I've found a few staples that will get me through any ritual. It really is okay to substitute if you genuinely can't get hold of something. My top three essentials are:

1. **Frankincense:** in resin form, this can be used in any purification spell, and its protective powers always come in handy.

2. **Sandalwood:** this comes in either chips or powder form. It also has protective and purification powers, and can be substituted for any missing ingredient in healing spells.

3. **Dragon's Blood:** this comes in powder form, and can be used for purification and protection. It's also an important ingredient for spells that focus on love energy.

With these three, you can cover most spell and ritual needs. Of course, having a well-stocked witch's cupboard is a bit addictive; so most witches I know have far more than they ever need. Me included.

✑ Ways to Use Herbs ✑

Charms and sachets: fill a small fabric or cotton teabag with herbs to make a charm or sachet. You can carry the charm with you, hang it in the house or car, bury it or burn it, depending on the purpose and the spell you're performing.

Incense: you can also burn herbs as a ritual incense; for example sage smudge can clear negative vibrations from a space.

Bath: make a sachet and place it in your ritual or healing bath. Fragrant herbs like lavender make a very relaxing bath, and you can use certain other herbs to alleviate various conditions, such as eucalyptus when you have a cold or flu.

Oils: place your herbs in an oil and let them steep for a few days, then strain. You can make anointing oils for your ritual work; beauty oils for your hair, skin and nails (try coconut or jojoba); or flavoured oils for cooking and seasoning (try steeping rosemary in olive oil).

Teas: use herbs to make teas to heal illness (but read the medical disclaimer below first). Some herbs can also be used to mildly alter consciousness, such as Valerian or Kava Kava, which can both facilitate trance-like states in some people. Teas are my most favourite ways to work with herbs, and my nanna was the queen of herbal tea making.

Spell work: sprinkle herbs or place them around or within boundaries (such as your home, altar, or magic circle) to define a 'territory' for your magic to work.

Cooking: obviously, you can also use flavourful herbs in cooking and seasoning your food. There are many health benefits, and they taste great.

✑✑✑

NOTE

If a plant can be used as medicine, that means it causes specific changes in your body. And that, in turn, means that taking too high a dose, taking it regularly for too long or taking it when you're also taking other herbs, supplements or medications may be dangerous.

If you're already taking medication of any kind, please speak to a qualified herbal medicine practitioner before using any of these herbs internally.

Additionally, certain herbs can affect different people in different ways. If you try taking a herb internally and experience unwanted side effects, stop taking it immediately and consult a qualified herbal medicine practitioner before taking it again.

Finally, the following information is NOT a substitute for medical diagnosis by a qualified professional. If you're in pain or discomfort, or have any other physical, mental or emotional symptom that persists, please talk to a doctor or qualified herbal medicine practitioner.

Finally, respect all plant life, wherever you are.

Remember that the word 'weed' is simply a judgement. Dandelion, for instance, has many, many healing and nutritional qualities, which are extremely beneficial not only to the wildlife that feeds on it, but also to you too.

Learn to recognize the wide variety of herbs around you. Even in a city, there are many herbs growing wild that you can gather and use.

Herbs are Mumma Nature's gift – use them with love and wisdom.

A Witch's Herbal

These are some of my most used and go-to herbs: I recommend keeping them on your witch shelf for healing, tinctures, teas and spell work.

Camphor

A pain reliever that heals skin – camphor is especially good for the lips and nose, and for burns. Sacred to the Goddess, it's used in full moon rituals as an offering to Her. Also use it for purification, promoting celibacy and heightening physical energy.

Catnip

This herb treats colds, reduces fever, aids indigestion and curbs flatulence. It also strengthens the psychic bond between humans and animals; and you can use it for courage, true love and lasting happiness.

Cayenne

A very important first aid herb, cayenne feels hot, but doesn't burn the skin or inner tissues. It helps to coagulate blood, both internally and externally, so can be sprinkled directly onto a bleeding cut. It's also good for heart disease.

Chamomile

Soothing to the body and mind, chamomile makes a good sedative tea before bed, and a mild pain-relieving compress. Use it for good luck (or to change your luck), to prevent lightning strikes to your house or person, for prosperity and as a meditation aid.

Clove

This spice can ease toothache, calm stomach pain and relieve gas. Clove can also banish hostility or negative energy, increase personal gain, clear a cloudy mind and increase friendship or love.

Coltsfoot

Often used for pain relief, and to suppress allergies and coughs, coltsfoot is also good for wealth, prosperity and love spells.

Comfrey

Very nutritious to eat, comfrey also soothes the stomach, and heals sprains, strains, fractures, sores and arthritis. Use it in protection spells and for safety when travelling.

Damiana

An aphrodisiac herb, damiana also improves digestion and relieves coughs. Use it in sex magic spells, and for clairvoyance and divination.

Devil's shoestring

Use devil's shoestring for protection, luck, a pay rise or a new job. You can also use it in invisibility spells.

Fennel

A digestive aid, fennel can be chewed or brewed as a tea for weight loss, gas relief and halitosis. It also imparts strength and sexual virility, and prevents curses.

Galangal root

Use galangal to cleanse your system internally, or take it at the onset of a cold or flu. Magically, use it to double your money in gambling, to win in court, or for sex magic, hex breaking and to aid psychic powers.

Garlic

Good for your hair, skin, digestion, lungs and blood health, garlic can also lower cholesterol and blood pressure. It's good for ear infections, and can heal colds and flu. Tincture it by steeping in olive oil, then use it for magical healing, protection and exorcism.

Ginger

Use ginger as relaxing stimulant, or after large meals to settle your stomach. It can induce perspiration if you're sweating out a fever, and aid the liver. It's also a powerful aphrodisiac when sprinkled in steeping raspberry-leaf tea.

Ginseng

Several different – and not always related – herbs go by the name 'ginseng' (e.g. Korean, Siberian, Indian and American), and each one has different healing properties. However, most types of ginseng help your body to adapt to stress, and promote longevity. Some also have anti-depressant properties, especially if used with St. John's wort; while others can improve stamina, balance hormones and assist with digestion.

Use ginseng magically in spells for love, beauty and healing.

Heal all

As the name suggests, this herb helps with all-purpose healing. Gargle cold tea for a sore throat, or use it as a poultice for cuts, abrasions and minor contusions. You can also use it in spells for success in gambling.

Hibiscus

This anti-spasmodic is also a remedy for itchy-skin or mild hives: just apply the fresh tea or tonic to your skin. It also sweetens your breath and attracts love; and you can use it for dream work or divination.

High John the Conqueror

Use this herb to conquer any situation; as well as for good luck, money, love, health, protection and to find lost items.

Jasmine

This sweet-smelling flower calms nervous tics, and makes a healing poultice for snakebite. It also attracts money and love, and you can use it for divination, charging crystals and moon magic.

Kava Kava

If Kava Kava is legal where you live, it can be a powerful aphrodisiac. Use it in potions to induce visions, for astral travel work or for protection in travelling.

Lavender

This herb is pretty much ALL PURPOSE. Use it for stomach problems, nausea and vomiting (as a tonic); and for healing, inner peace, peace of mind, relieving stress, finding love, money, protection, attracting good spirits and faeries, purification, peaceful sleep and headache relief. Inhaling the oil can also relieve menstrual cramps.

Mugwort

This appetite stimulant and digestive aid can also help with visions, dreams, clairvoyance, protection and strength in travelling. Use it to consecrate divination tools, and to add or boost power in tools of scrying.

Patchouli

Patchouli can reverse spells and peacefully get rid of troublemakers. Use it in clairvoyance, divination, sex magic and to manifest and draw money.

Pennyroyal

CAUTION: USE IN SMALL DOSES ONLY, AND NEVER IN PREGNANCY

A form of mint, pennyroyal can repel insects, and calm both skin itches and nervous itches. Use it to treat and soothe nausea, or treat colds and flu. You can also use it in consecration rituals and exorcisms.

Peppermint

Another mint, peppermint soothes nausea (including motion sickness), upset stomachs and heartburn, and is also good for colds and flu. It's calming, and can promote peaceful sleep and visionary dreams as well as boosting psychic abilities.

Plantain

A blood detoxifier, plantain can treat poison ivy, snakebite, bee stings, mosquito bites, etc. Crush the leaves, apply their juice to bites and stings, and then reapply it often. Alternatively, drink a tea brewed from the leaves, or eat and chew on fresh leaves.

Raspberry leaf

Use this herb for kidney strength, and to help treat infections, diarrhoea, nausea, colds and flu. It makes a calming nerve tonic, and is useful for preparing the uterus for childbirth in late pregnancy (use only under supervision). It also promotes peaceful sleep, and can be used for visionary work, protection and love spells.

Rosemary

This nerve stimulant and digestive aid also helps with memory and soothes headaches, and the scent can ease depression. Use it for protection, exorcisms, purification, healing and to stimulate lust. It's also a powerful herb to add to any incense to help it burn and create smoke.

Rose hips

Very nutritious as well as tasty, rose hips are high in Vitamin C. Take them for colds or flu, and to reduce fever. They're also mildly laxative, and good for acne. Use them for spells concerning good luck, or to summon good spirits.

Sage

Use sage as an antiperspirant and to help heal wounds. It aids digestion and relieves muscle and joint pain, and it's particularly good for menopausal night sweats and perspiration from hot flushes. Gargle sage tea to heal mouth and gum sores; and drink it to heal colds and flu, and reduce fever. Use it in spells for wisdom, healing, money, protection and longevity. It's also a powerful herb to use in ritual incense.

Sandalwood

Use sandalwood as a poultice for bruises and minor contusions, and to reduce fever. Magically, use it in clairvoyance and protection spells, and for purification and meditation. Burn it in rituals to aid in magical work, stimulate sexual urges, and aid in healing spells.

Skullcap

A tranquillizing and sleep-promoting herb, skullcap is classed as a mild to moderate sedative. It eases nervous tension, drug and alcohol withdrawal symptoms and premenstrual pain. It also relieves anxiety and promotes relaxation and peaceful feelings.

St. John's wort

Use St John's wort to heal wounds and boost your immune system. It also helps with insomnia, relieves headaches, eases menstrual cramps and can be used as a mood enhancer (it's a powerful anti-depressant). Use it for protection, exorcism, courage and divination rituals.

Valerian

Try valerian to calm your nerves, aid sleep and treat nervous conditions. It also helps to calm spasms, and reduces blood pressure. Use it in love magic, purification, divination and black magic.

Vervain

Use vervain for minor pains, headaches, toothaches, arthritis and other inflammations. It's also good for restful sleep and calming your nerves. Magically, you can use it for protection, purification and consecration, and in potions for love and creativity.

Tea Medicine

> *'Tea began as a medicine and grew into a beverage.'*
> - OKAKURA KAKUZŌ

My nanna was obsessed with making tea. She had a recipe to heal EVERYTHING, and now I know why. Teas are a really easy way to access the health benefits of herbs.

When I held a retreat last year, one of the women who heard The Call and joined me was Clare Fairhurst. Every morning, I'd watch her bring these beautiful tubes of herbs to the kitchen and go about her quiet ritual of delicately preparing and sipping a cup of tea.

When the retreat ended, I took my prompt from Clare, and I too turned tea drinking into both medicine and a ritual. I pulled out my nanna's herbal, bought a beautiful glass teapot with small, hold-in-the-palm-of-your-hand-size cups and began to remember.

Now I often hear the whispers of my nanna as I sip the warm herbal mixtures I concoct for menstrual pain, for nerve soothing and for energy boosting. The whole practice of making and drinking tea has now become something quite beautiful.

My most frequently used recipe is my nanna's cure for menstrual cramps and womb soothing (you can find that in my book *Love Your Lady Landscape*). However, I also really love a tea that she used to make whenever I was feeling snotty, or my immune system needed a boost.

I've rather cleverly, if I do say so myself, named it Immuni-tea.

See what I did there?

∽ Immuni-Tea ∾

Use 1 part of each herb for this blend. A part can be anything from a teaspoon to a cup, depending on how much you want to make. I use dried herbs.

What you'll need:

- 1 part elderberries
- 1 part elderflowers
- 1 part chamomile
- 1 part rose hips
- 1 part echinacea

Simply mix all the herbs together, and store in an airtight container.

To brew:

Use 1 tsp of your Immuni-Tea blend per cup of hot water, and steep for at least 20 minutes (or overnight for a more potent herbal infusion).

If you're keeping the tea loose, strain it through a strainer and sweeten with honey for additional healing properties. You could also sweeten it with stevia (you can add it as a herb to the blend, or as a liquid), or leave it unsweetened.

❧

This tea is safe for all ages and tastes really good hot or cold. However, if you have an autoimmune disease, you should be cautious when using **any** immune-stimulating herb.

I Heart Damiana

I can't talk about tea without sharing my most favourite herb (I'm a witch, so of course I've got a favourite herb!) If you don't know about damiana, you NEED to.

The indigenous people of Mexico have known for a LONG time that damiana is a potent and popular aphrodisiac. Oh yeah.

In Mexico today, it's frequently dispensed in the form of a herbal liqueur. The liqueur is prepared by steeping damiana, along with vanilla, galangal, cinnamon and pimento berries in honey and rum for about two weeks.

According to some, sprinkling damiana on the food of the one you love will intensify desire. Others use it in a herbal bath to attract new love. It's also said that if you carry damiana in a mojo bag, your straying lover will return to you. (Whether you'll want them back or not is an entirely different matter.)

Personally, I've found it to be super-relaxing, providing almost instant feel-good vibes; and that makes sense, since, in its native country, damiana was traditionally used as a tonic for worn-out nerves and depression.

I also find it great for opening me up during dreamtime and meditation. Although, I won't lie, dreamtime can get a little erotic if you drink it before bed. Wink.

And finally – as if you're not already in LOVE with this herb – damiana is also one of the best herbs for women's health, *especially* for those of us who experience cramps, irritability and mood swings around our period.

Damiana, we love you.

✑ DAMIANA TEA ✑

Steep 2 tsp of damiana in boiling water for 5–10 minutes.

Add honey, maybe some dried rosebuds for some extra love and healing, and enjoy warm.

Essential Oils

Essential oils and their potent aromatic gifts have seriously ancient origins. Translations of Ancient Egyptian hieroglyphs show that alchemists were using extracted oils from plants and herbs for healing, ritual and ceremony thousands of years ago. The pharaohs of Ancient Egypt routinely exchanged blue lotus oil with the kings of India for gold and other precious goods. Yep, there was a time when essential oils were considered as valuable as gold.

While they have long been revered for their ability to provide healing and rejuvenation, there is now growing clinical evidence that essential oils – the pure, high-quality ones extracted from the barks, roots, stems, flowers, berries and leaves of various plants – contain wellbeing and therapeutic benefits for the body, mind and emotions.

Using essential oils

Essential oils are highly concentrated, which means you usually only need a drop or two to make magic (although I've been known to get seriously carried away with rose absolute in the bath – just call me Cleopatra).

I recommend sniffing lots of different oils and getting to know the ones you like (and the ones you definitely don't like, too). Then look up their particular qualities and benefits so that you can start to create a set of go-to oils for your personal use. As long as you store them in airtight containers in a cool, dark place, they'll last for years.

However, make sure you know the source of your oils. The synthetic fragrance industry is growing, and many of the essential oils available today are diluted with carrier oils and synthetic fragrances. Not only does this decrease the therapeutic and healing potency of the oil, it may also mean the oil you're using contains other toxic nasties. So be aware. Make sure the oils you buy have been tested by a reliable, independent, qualified laboratory and are certified to be pure and therapeutically potent, and not just to smell good.

Essential Oils and Their Magical Properties	
Anise	Psychic awareness, clairvoyance
Basil	Conscious mind, happiness, peace, money-attraction
Bergamot	Peace, happiness, restful sleep, stress soothing
Black Pepper	Mental alertness, physical energy, protection, courage
Cedarwood	Spirituality, self-control, healing, anti-hex
Cinnamon	Physical energy, protection, psychic awareness, prosperity, healing
Clary Sage	Euphoria, calming, dreams
Clove Bud	Healing, memory, protection, courage
Coffee	Conscious mind, breaking deadlocks
Cypress	Easing and comforting losses, healing, blessing, consecration

Dragon's Blood	Protection, purification, love
Eucalyptus	Health, healing, purification
Frankincense	Spirituality, meditation, astral strength
Geranium	Happiness, protection, power in ritual and magic
Ginger	Magical energy, physical energy, sex, love, money-attraction, courage
Grapefruit	Purification
Hyssop	Purification, conscious mind
Jasmine	Love, calming, peace, spirituality, sex, sleep, psychic dreaming
Lavender	Health, love, peace, relaxing
Lemon	Energizing, health, healing, physical energy, purification
Lemongrass	Psychic awareness, purification
Lime	Purification, physical energy, protection
Lotus	Spirituality, healing, meditation, opening, elevating
Marjoram	Peace, celibacy, sleep
Mugwort	Psychic awareness, psychic dreams, astral projection
Myrrh	Spirituality, meditation, healing
Orange	Purification, joy, physical energy, magical energy
Patchouli	Sex, money, physical energy
Peppermint	Conscious mind, purification
Pine	Healing, purification, protection, physical energy, money, magical energy
Rosemary	Longevity, memory, love, conscious mind, healing, purification

Rose	Love, peace, sex, beauty
Sage	Memory, wisdom, money, purification
Sandalwood	Spirituality, healing, purification, meditation
Spearmint	Healing, protection during sleep
Tangerine	Wellbeing, wards off psychic and social vampires, adds power to mixtures
Tea tree	Harmony
Vanilla	Sex, love, physical energy, magical energy
Vetiver(t)	Protection, money, unhexing
Wintergreen	Protection of animals, good luck, money
Wormwood	Aphrodisiac, clairvoyance, spell-breaking, love, anything psychically related
Ylang-Ylang	Love, peace, sex

Crystals and Caring for Them

I know, I know. Crystals aren't herbs. But these precious gifts from Mumma Earth contain potent healing properties, and definitely belong in your witch's medicine bag.

Crystals sometimes get ridiculed for being overused New Age crutches, but ancient cultures have always held them sacred, believing them to store and hold secrets and messages, and using them in meditation and for healing.

Today, scientists and techno geeks the world over use the power held in rocks and crystals in everything from watches and computers to laser technology.

Crystals are from Mumma Earth, and in magical and spell work, a wand is often topped with a crystal to amplify its conjuring and manifestation abilities. You can also place crystals on an object to clear blockages. For example, I place a piece of carnelian on my womb if I'm suffering from menstrual cramps. They can be used to communicate with the dead, as well as in divination. They're basically spiritual multitaskers.

When you buy crystals, try to get them in as natural a form as possible. If they're all smooth and round, they'll usually have been treated with chemicals and tumbled in a violent way that's supposed to enhance their colour and uniformity. Personally, though, I like them in their more raw and natural forms.

These are my most loved and used crystals, and what I use them for.

Amethyst

A natural stress reliever, amethyst encourages inner strength, and brings wealth and a strong business sense to its wearer.

It's a crystal of spiritual growth and protection that brings mental clarity, and helps you to become more in tune with your feelings and know yourself on a much deeper level.

Amethyst crystals repel negative energy and attract positive energy, making them a wonderful protection stone for your home. In fact, they're one of the strongest crystals for ridding your home of negative influences.

Bloodstone

Healers for thousands of years have valued bloodstone's powerful healing energy. It can purify and detoxify your body, grounding negative energy and cleansing your body's own energy.

Bloodstone also increases energy and strength, promoting constant energy flow throughout the body. It's very beneficial for athletes and people whose jobs involve a lot of physical activity.

Carnelian

A powerful sacral chakra stone, carnelian increases personal power and physical energy, bringing you courage, compassion and a boost in creativity.

Wearing or carrying carnelian enhances vitality and will, providing you with the confidence needed to approach new projects and dreams. It's also a wonderful stone to wear on a job interview, as it brings good luck and opportunity, awakening your hidden talents within.

In ancient times, Egyptians buries their loved ones with carnelian because they thought it protected the dead in their journey to the afterlife, and calmed their fears about rebirth.

Chrysocolla

A very peaceful stone that soothes and calms during stressful times, chrysocolla connects with your throat chakra, helping you to consciously express yourself.

It gently draws off negative energies of all kinds, especially in times of transition, such as breakups or job loss. It's wonderful to wear on a daily basis as a support stone or to help calm your emotions. Chrysocolla also helps you to face challenges and changes with ease, inspires inner balance and self-awareness, and increases your capacity to love.

Citrine

A stone of light and happiness, citrine doesn't hold any negative energy, so it never needs cleansing. Wearing it brings clarity, and helps you to manifest anything you want to bring into your life.

It activates your imagination, bringing more creative visions to a clearer mind and a more positive outlook in life. Powered by the sun, citrine warms, cleanses and energizes your body, in particular energizing and strengthening your solar plexus.

Clear quartz

Clear quartz is a stone of manifestation that energizes and activates the energy centres within your body. It helps you to think clearly, allowing you to focus and get clear about your dreams and desires. Assisting with spiritual development, clear quartz helps to remove blockages in your body so that energy can flow smoothly.

Garnet

A stone of health and energy, garnet enhances passion and pleasure. It helps to move the chi and energy within the body, stimulating physical activity.

Garnet is also a good stone to help with depression, as it brings joy and hope, and helps to lessen any anger you direct at yourself. It also cleanses the chakras of negative energy, re-energizing them in the process.

Hematite

Hematite is a very protective stone that helps you to stay grounded in any situation. It absorbs negative energy and calms you in times of stress or worry. Wearing hematite helps you to feel balanced, calm and centred. This stone also helps you to find your own unique talents and release self-imposed limitations.

Jade

Considered a powerful lucky charm, jade can help you attain your goals and dreams. It allows you to see past self-imposed limitations and manifest your dreams into the physical world.

Jade also promotes courage, compassion, generosity and longevity, helping you lead a richer, more fulfilling life. It's a gemstone with much history, having been part of Asian history for centuries.

Jasper

Highly valued as a healing stone, jasper is full of grounding energy. It can connect you deeply to the vibrations of the Earth, bringing a greater understanding of the power of nature. Jasper helps you to be less judgemental and know on a soul level that we are all connected.

In some Native American cultures, jasper symbolizes the blood of the Earth, making it particularly sacred.

Labradorite

Labradorite cleans and opens your crown chakra by stimulating your intuition. It's a power stone that allows you to see through illusions and determine the actual form of your dreams and goals. Use labradorite to stimulate your imagination, develop enthusiasm and see more clearly in meditation.

Lapis lazuli

Having existed since the beginning of time, lapis lazuli is a gemstone of total awareness that connects you to a higher truth. It helps to foster verbal expression, opening and balancing your throat chakra.

It also provides wisdom and connects you to your spiritual guardians, shielding you from negative energy and returning any negative vibrations back to their source.

Malachite

A stone of transformation, malachite helps to clear and cleanse all the chakras. It's an overall healing stone that stimulates and balances your heart and throat chakras.

Malachite also helps you to release negative experiences so you can heal and refuel on hope. It's inspiring, purifying and compassionate, and attracts love by opening your heart.

Moonstone

Believed to be a stone of destiny, moonstone is strongly connected to the moon and the Divine Feminine, making it a wonderfully helpful stone for women. It's worn to increase fertility and harmonize the mind, providing health and protection.

Moonstone helps to align hormone production, metabolism and reproduction. It also allows deep-rooted feelings to energize and come to the fore.

Obsidian

Obsidian is a natural volcanic glass formed from molten lava that has cooled very rapidly. It's a grounding stone that provides an instant connection from the root chakra deep into the core of the Earth.

Obsidian also helps to clean and remove negative energies; and helps to release emotions that cause negative energy such as anger, fear, jealousy and greed.

Onyx

A powerful protective stone that can shield your mind and body from electromagnetic energy, onyx absorbs and transforms negative energy, and helps to prevent personal energy drain.

It also assists with melancholy, releases negativity and depression and helps to calm your fears – leaving you feeling stable and secure.

Rose quartz

Rose quartz is the stone of unconditional love. It's one of the most important stones for heart chakra work, as it opens your heart to all types of love – self-love, love of family, love of friends and romantic love.

The soothing energy of rose quartz fosters empathy, reconciliation and forgiveness of others, lowering heart-based stress and tension. It can clear out anger, jealousy and resentment towards others, allowing heart issues caused by holding on to negative emotions to heal.

Selenite

The ideal crystal for all types of energy clearing, selenite can clear, protect and shield your energy body as well as clearing the energy of your other crystals and home. It quickly unblocks any stagnant or negative energy to create a smooth flow of positive energy.

Selenite crystals magnify the energy of any other gemstone that is placed upon them, making this stone perfect for reactivating and recharging your jewellery and other healing crystals. It has also been recently used in holistic medicine treatments for physical healing, including cancer treatment and tumour reduction.

Smoky quartz

Smoky quartz helps to ground and connect you to the Earth, allowing you to keep your feet on the ground and remain balanced. It emits a high level of energy that absorbs and transmutes negative energy.

Smoky quartz helps to remove mental and emotional blockages, relieving pain and dispersing negative energy from your body. Wear it for emotional support, and to dissolve anger and resentment.

Tiger's eye

Helping to rebalance your body on all levels, tiger's eye encourages optimism and trust in the future. It brings brightness and light into all situations and shines insight onto all problems.

Wearing tiger's eye also brings good luck, abundance and prosperity. In many ancient civilizations, it was used as a talisman against bad luck and curses; and it's a must-have in any home for healing.

Cleansing Your Crystals

If you buy your crystal from a shop, there's a chance that it's been handled by lots of other people, who've all left their energetic fingerprints on it. Purifying and charging your crystals will bring them to a neutral state and clear any negative vibes. Use your intuition and let it guide you.

⟶ THREE STEPS TO CLEANSE ⟵
YOUR CRYSTALS

1. Cleanse your crystal by holding it under running water (tap water or river) for a few minutes.

2. Re-energize your crystal in the sunlight and moonlight (preferably the full moon) for either 24 hours, three days or seven days – you'll know what feels right.

3. Repeat your chosen process anytime you feel the stone needs recharging, usually a few months later.

Don't place in water any crystal that's attached to metal jewellery. Instead, burn sage and pass the jewellery through the smoke.

Alternatively, leave the jewellery on a big piece of amethyst for 24 hours.

Charging/Programming Your Crystals

Each crystal already has its own list of magical properties – everything from attracting love and abundance to healing period pain and helping you to communicate. However, you can also programme your crystal or charge it to amplify its purpose.

∽ How to Programme/ ⌒ Charge Your Crystals

1. Decide what purpose you want your crystal to have. Are you going to use it for meditation? To help you focus? To heal a broken heart?

2. Once you've decided, hold your crystal with your dominant hand and imagine a bright white light coming up from your womb and circulating round your body, before it reaches the crystal and fills it with your light-infused power.

3. Thank the crystal for all the ways it's going to help you. For example, you could say, 'Thank you for the love in my heart/for how clearly I'm able to speak in public/how happy I feel.'

Other methods

The sun. Of course, the sun is a very powerful energizer: use it whenever possible to dry your crystals. You can also let your stones simply soak in the sun, letting them rest in the light.

The Earth. Bury the stone under the earth in your garden to effectively cleanse your stone of all its negativity.

A quartz crystal. Place your stone on a large quartz crystal cluster for a few hours to quickly neutralize any negative energies within your stone.

∽⊙⌒

Figure Out What Works for You

Use my witch's herbal as a starting place, then begin to create your own.

As you try out recipes, create spells, combine oils and work with crystals, start to write down what you're creating them for. Write down when you created each thing, which ingredients you used, what worked and what didn't, and under which moon phase you created it.

Discover new herbs, oils and crystals and their properties, and allow yourself to be guided. Most importantly, trust yourself as you explore.

Trust: The Final Ingredient

Guess what? We have EVERYTHING we need to heal.

When I used to spend Saturday mornings with my nanna, she'd invite me to make teas and tinctures based on whichever herbs I was called to. I didn't know their medical or magical properties, but I used to have fun taking a spoon out of one jar and placing it into another. We both used to drink whatever concoction I'd make, and while it didn't always taste great, the healing quality of the herbs my nan had gathered for me to choose from meant that it was always good for us in one way or another.

I know now that she was getting me to flex my intuitive muscle and trust my teachers: plants, elders and – most importantly – myself. I'm grateful because it's this trust and intuition-flexing that I now use daily when I place a hand on a woman's womb space and instinctively know that her right ovary isn't working because of a trauma she experienced when she was six.

Or when I hear a woman describe her challenging menstrual experience and know that when I 'see' she's having trouble with her relationship, the two are NOT mutually exclusive.

More importantly, because I trust myself and my teachers, I also then know which movement, medicine or spiritual practice to offer her in order to help and heal.

When you reconnect with the wise woman – *She Who Knows* – as well as your ancestors and all those who've gone before, you become a powerful and potent healer.

You are a Healer.

I am a Healer.

The 'Wake the Witch' Project

Ways to invoke SHE Who Heals Herself and Heals the World:

Go on a herb walk: go walking in nature, and take or draw pictures of the plants that you find. Then get geeky and find out what they are, and what they can be used for.

Find a herbalist near where you live who offers seasonal herb walks or foraging lessons: it's an education in Mumma Nature.

Don't be afraid to question anything: in fact, question EVERYTHING. If you read that a specific herb is great for attracting love, but you hold it in your hand close to your heart, and it whispers a different meaning to you, trust yourself. If you're told in dreamtime to combine two kinds of herbs to make a tea, try it.

Be safe and take radical self-responsibility, but also trust your intuition.

Know that medicine can come in ALL forms: it's not just herbs, massage and essential oils. In fact, feeling medicine is by far my greatest teacher.

Allowing yourself to FEEL, no matter how painful a situation may be, can provide the most potent healing medicine you will *ever* experience.

Reading this book may hold emotional medicine for you as you remember your own true nature as a witch. Meanwhile, the dis-ease of an illness or chronic physical pain you're experiencing may be the medicine you need (not necessarily the one you want) to help you to return to your body.

Chapter 12

The Sorceress

*SHE Who Is Charmed,
Dangerous and Not
Afraid of the Dark*

Welcome to
the rewilding.

'*Where there is woman, there is magic.*'

— Ntozake Shange

One of my first online businesses was as *The Sassy Sorceress*. I made natural perfumes with crystals and essential oils, and charged them under the moon. These essences had names like *Charmed and Dangerous* (you can find the recipe on page 249), and they came with spells and an incantation. I also did online tarot readings, and ran imaginatively titled 'how-to-learn-the-tarot' witch classes.

I had no idea at the time of the potency of the title I'd given myself. SASSY stands for Spiritual, Authentic, Sensual, Sensational You (I LOVE an acronym!), and it's still very much at the core of everything I do and share.

But Sorceress? I'll be honest: that was a role I was trying out for size.

At the time, I'd just come out of an eight-year relationship where I wasn't supported, respected or honoured; and I wanted to experience being the Sorceress instead.

The stereotype version. The Angelina Jolie version.

The dark and dangerous version. The sexy, wild, someone-who'd-steal-your-partner-in-a-heartbeat version.

I know now that that version was warped, outdated and part of an old paradigm. But by taking the name 'Sorceress', I met her – in the same way as you do when you take on the word 'witch'.

Eye to eye.

Boobs to boobs.

Womb to womb.

Truth to truth.

I'd felt her powers before. Hell yes, I'd felt them. I'm a Scorpio, of course I'd felt them. Sometimes they'd even spilled over, and I'd dared to use them – like that time I took a trip to Paris with my BFF, and we kissed pretty men after having read too much Anaïs Nin (FYI: You can never read too much Anaïs Nin).

And after the eight-year relationship ended, I decided I'd no longer seek a husband. I'd take lovers instead. Lots of lovers.

But as I experimented with seduction and allure, pleasure and desire, I was called out. I was slapped (literally on occasions) back into line for daring to explore and meet *my* needs and desires on *my* terms.

Patriarchy, on witnessing the opening of Pandora's box, wanted me to shut the lid, (and my legs) and remain tame and compliant.

But Pandora literally means 'giver of all gifts'. And when you meet the Sorceress, she dares you to open Pandora's box (and your legs), because she knows that it's where her powers lie.

It's where YOUR power lies.

Yep, your power lies between your thighs. And when you connect with your lady landscape – your womb, your vulva, your clitoris, your ovaries, your desire and pleasure – you realize that the traits you'd been taught were 'wrong' and 'unacceptable' for a 'good girl like you' are all gifts to help you reclaim your power, authority and wholeness.

So yes, the Sorceress has the ability to change situations and 'manipulate'. *She's an alchemist. She's the mother who turns tears into laughter with a reassuring kiss. The friend who turns fear into ease with her words. The activist who changes thought into action.*

Yes, she can use her power to serve herself. *She knows that when she serves herself, she's full and whole and able to serve SHE and the world.*

Yes, she gets angry and rage-full and wild. *She knows that holding it in and pushing it down serves no one, least of all herself.*

Yes, she's comfortable in the dark. *She knows it's the only way truly to serve the light.*

Yes, she's sexy, alluring and able to seduce. *She's a woman, and it's her bloody prerogative to be.*

And guess what? You are SHE and SHE is you.

SHE asks – no, in fact SHE *demands* – that you claim these as gifts, instead of seeing them as the curses and evil and dangers that you've been taught that they are.

And SHE demands that you claim them *completely* unapologetically.

Who Is the Sorceress?

There's a new version of the Sorceress. It's actually the ancient version from BP (Before Patriarchy) – before the media recreated her in a way that made us all fear her. Sound familiar?

She represents you owning every single part of yourself: the so-called good and the bad, the dark and the light. And she represents using ALL of it to make sure you leave your footprints (and pussy-print), your legacy and your messy imperfections as a beautiful, deep, long-lasting impression of what it is to be a woman in her power on this planet.

> The Sorceress, with a heavy emphasis on the word 'source', is your reminder that YOU are source.

This isn't something you have to go out searching for, despite what you've been led to believe. Source is actually something you already are. It's something you can access at any given moment. And it's something you can use to transform, alchemize and integrate teachings, learnings, darkness and experiences.

THIS is the big, giant, humungous, ESSENTIAL, totally freaking *necessary* piece that Patriarchy has been trying to keep from us.

That we can totally transmute and alchemize experiences. We can change them up. Get all Kali Ma on their asses.

That our true, wild and seemingly uncontrollable nature (it's only uncontrollable to dude-kind: we on the other hand, just need a li'l practice to remember how to work WITH it) can experience, handle and be with it ALL.

The Sorceress – me and you – is the container for potent and powerful alchemy.

This is a force that we've been taught to fear instead of revere.

We want to be sexy, and feel confident and powerful… yet we don't want to be 'too' sexy. We don't want people to think we're sluts. (And by 'slut'? I mean, any woman who enjoys sex more than the man calling her it does.)

We don't want to be so confident that we come off as arrogant or a diva. We don't want to be so powerful that we offend someone, or – and this is the trickiest of them all – end up with *more* power than we can handle.

Witch, you can handle it. ALL OF IT. I promise.

Come into your body.

Rewilding the 'Source'ress

Take a deep breath, in through your nose and deep into your core.

Breathe into your cauldron, your pelvis, and fill *everything* it holds with *prana* (life force).

Yes, this is a place of manifesting and creation. But more importantly, it's home to your power source. And if you're not connected to that, the process of rewilding and reclamation as the Sorceress will rip you from your roots.

FYI: I speak from experience.

So witch, root down.

Come in. Into your body.

Right down to your roots, and breathe into them.

Allow the fire, anger and passion – the desire that you've been holding back and pushing down and medicating to avoid – to be there.

It's been ignored for FAR too long.

SHE's been ignored for too long.

You no longer need to be afraid of it.

Feel this truth in your very centre. Taste it, smell it, journal it, move with it, cry with it and tend to it.

The Sorceress IS rewilding.

It's a return to our core wildness.

It's a return to our true nature.

It's a return to the essence of who all witches are behind all the bullshit stories we believe about ourselves because we've been *told* that they're true.

This, ladylove, is the Sorceress, and SHE will fuel your rewilding.
What is rewilding?

Rewilding is reclaiming and returning to your wild, feminine nature. It's returning to:

… who you were before all the labels and conditionings were put on you like constrictive metal shackles.

… who you were when you didn't ignore your anger, passion and true feelings.

… who you were when you allowed those things to be fully felt and expressed IN and THROUGH your body.

Who you were when you surrendered to the FULL experience of being a woman.

When you say yes to the rewilding, you no longer look up to a higher being or go outside yourself for guidance. Instead, you make the conscious choice to turn inwards – to face yourself. You meet yourself eye to eye, boob to boob, womb to womb. You meet the shadows and the truths, and well...that?

That most definitely is witch work.

So many of us avoid that work, and I get why. It feels risky. Like you have to let go of an 'old' version of yourself, a false version that you've unknowingly believed to be your true self.

You have to look at all the habits, the behaviours, the things that you do to mask and medicate suppressed feelings. You have to meet the wounds – not just yours, but the collective wounds we spoke of earlier in Chapter 4.

The rewilding invites you into the cosmic womb, the dark sea of awareness, where you 'see' truth in the dark. And what you see is that underneath it all, underneath the labels and the bullshit stories, it's ALL LOVE.

ALL OF IT.

Except that, as you begin rewilding, if you've previously been very attached to your mask of 'love and light' (or 'glamour' or 'spirituality lite' or 'serving others' or 'ambition'), it won't feel like healing or love.

Instead, it will probably feel a lot like (and this is most definitely *my* personal experience) you're a massive fuck-up. It will feel like failure. It will feel really bloody messy.

Not only that, but people around you won't entirely know what to do with you either. Some will demand you stop what you're doing and return to your 'normal' self, because *they* feel uncomfortable. Or they'll claim, 'You've changed!'; and you'll then have to navigate the unspoken contracts you made with them to 'keep you safe'.

For me, writing and editing this book has been one *massive* rewilding process.

(Oh yeah: rewilding *isn't* a one-off process. It has layers and spirals and edges; and whenever you think you've got something figured out, you're given a different camera angle through which to view it. You WILL thank me for introducing you to it. Just... probably not right away.)

And as I've shared what I know and what's coming through to be seen and witnessed on these pages, I've unravelled. It has NOT made me fun to live with.

If you follow me on Instagram, you'll have witnessed this unravelling for yourself. It's been messy. And for women who've been tamed, censored and told as young girls to 'keep quiet, don't be seen and definitely don't cry', the unravelling, the spilling over and the being 'seen' as emotional and messy is a REALLY big ask.

If you experience a menstrual cycle, I invite you to explore rewilding in the premenstrual phase. Or if you don't bleed, explore it during the waning and darkness of the moon. Because it's during these times that our womanly wildness – our truth, our voice and our very essence in all its messy, imperfect glory – demands to be untamed and uncensored, to be seen and heard the most.

Now, if that actually happened? If we all took life by the ovaries and actually spilled our hearts, guts and wombs – without censorship – with the waning of the moon or the waning of our menstrual cycle? A heavily patriarchal structure like the one we currently live in would (and should) be scared shitless. Because as Audre Lorde, African American writer, feminist, womanist, lesbian and civil rights activist so rightly pointed out, we'd be 'powerful and dangerous'.

Except we wouldn't. Not really. We'd simply be bringing our real. Sharing from a place of womb-deep truth.

What feels *more* dangerous to me right now is that we've been taught to disown the power of the second half of our menstrual cycle, and yet this is where our fullest expression can be witnessed and experienced.

If the first half is a deep inhale, this half is the exhale. It's the letting go. The opportunity to let our hearts, guts and wombs lead us into a different, deeper way of 'being' instead of 'doing'.

Unfortunately, so many of us are totally disconnected from it. Why? Because this phase can get a little messy. And as modern women, we learn very early on to keep the 'messy' aspects of our femininity under wraps. Our emotions, should they spill out, get squashed – and we apologize. A LOT.

We worry that we're being seen as 'too much', while at the same time struggling with feeling like we're 'not enough'. We're scared to come undone, because how will we ever put it all back together again?

Well, guess what? You don't *have* to.

That cosmic womb I spoke about? That sea of awareness? If you let it, it'll dissolve anything and everything that isn't love. When *that* happens, you'll start to get really comfortable with outbursts of passion, anger, grief, desire and fire. You'll become wild, outspoken and truthful.

THIS is rewilding.

Know, though, that it takes courage and vulnerability to take that first step. There'll be a 'not knowing', where you'll wonder how you'll be judged and perceived. Because standing in your power, no matter what – expressing yourself, creating on *your* terms, knowing what you want and trusting that who you are is *exactly* what's needed?

THAT takes bloody big ovaries.

Yet this is the very essence of the Sorceress. It's being your true self. Unleashed. Untamed. Unapologetic. In every given moment.

And you begin the journey – the spiral, the adventure – by exploring your lady landscape.

Access the Magic in Your Cauldron

The Sorceress knows that while fancy tools and equipment are great, she has everything she ACTUALLY needs to make magic already inside her.

Literally.

Her pelvic bowl – and the womb and ovaries that reside within it – is an in-built cauldron of creativity. It's a medicine bowl, an oracle, a place to heal and transmute it ALL.

When your ovaries are nurtured – fully charged and circulating with energy – you can use them to create and express yourself in ALL THE WAYS.

When you stir your cauldron – through dance, sound, movement and breath – you connect with an inner power source. That source is like an internal ignition switch: something the ancient yogis called Shakti. Shakti is divine feminine energy that, when activated, allows you to express yourself fully and creatively.

You feel fertile in ALL the ways.

And you *are*. Basically, be aware that you have the capacity to create ANYTHING when you stir and activate Shakti in your cauldron: babies, magic, relationships, projects and yes, orgasms.

Of course, with great creative power comes great creative responsibility.

Act accordingly.

Create epic shit. PLEASE. The world needs you to create ALL the things in ALL the ways.

Shakti Rising

Shakti is life-force energy.

In her fundamental essence, Shakti is uncontrollable. She's the wildest, most feral rattlesnake sort of energy that I've ever encountered.

She cannot and will not be tamed.

She's what you and I feel like when we *totally* surrender to the process of rewilding.

People who work with Shakti sometimes think they're harnessing or controlling her, but Shakti is the fuel that powers all of creation. She fuels the universe, the planet and individual beings. She *cannot* be harnessed or controlled.

Her energy is pure potential, and all that's required from you is to stand in the centre and trust that you have this infinite creative force moving through you.

SHE is you and you are SHE.

Connect with Shakti, connect with the witch.

☙ Connect with Shakti ❧

Stand up and plug your toes into the motherboard. Put your bare feet on the actual earth if you can, because the soles of your feet are one of three convergence points on the body for your seventy-two thousand nerve fibres.

When you place bare feet on the ground, each of those nerve fibres connects with the pulse of Mumma Earth and conducts electromagnetic energy through your body.

Take in a breath; and on the exhale, send your roots down into Mumma Earth. Then, on the next inhale, feel her energy come right back up at you and into your womb. Do this for three to five powerful breaths.

Then let her move you.

Let her be your guide.

As you move to the rhythm of your own flow, ask, 'What do I really want? What is my desire?'

This will probably bring 'stuff' up for you: 'I can't trust my desire.' 'I mess up.' 'I get greedy.' 'I want nice things – car/house/money.'

Allow any emotion that needs to be witnessed to be fully felt and seen – scream, cry, laugh, sob – and then journal and process what's come up for you.

I do this process in each phase of my menstrual cycle, but you can do it at the full moon, or the dark moon or even daily.

Just know that the more you practise connecting with Shakti, the more you'll be able to trust your body as a messenger.

༺ঔৣ༻

The Sorceress invites you to work with Shakti to unravel.

Yes, it's safe for you to unravel.

It's safe for you to unravel.

If it doesn't feel safe for you, join my online SHE coven: details are in the resources section at the back of the book. All of us need –

more than anything – to have safe, courageous places, spaces and containers in which it feels safe for us to unravel. Places, spaces and containers where we can start to practise exploring the light AND the dark with other women.

For many of us, there's a LOT of dark attached to the idea of being raw and vulnerable with other women. To admit a perceived vulnerability or weakness. To declare, 'Look, I haven't got my shit together. My life *isn't* always as shiny as it might appear on social media.' But the trust between women that Patriarchy has broken over the last 3,000 years by separating us from each other and tuning us against each other, needs rebuilding.

And that rebuilding starts with us.

Wisdom is Held in the Dark

The problem is, that being taught/required/forced to live 100 per cent in the light has made us forget the wisdom that's held in the dark. Let me use the menstrual cycle as an example.

Each month, like the moon, you experience the light *and* the dark. The first half of your cycle is the pre-ovulation and ovulation phase, when you're energized and feel like you can do pretty much anything. The problem is that you're taught to show up this way *all* month: and you feel like you 'should' be able to stay this way all month long.

But you can't.

Because during the second half – the premenstrual and menstrual phases – our bodies literally *can't* sustain the same pace. That's why we yearn to rest and restore: physically, emotionally and spiritually.

That second half is the shadow side of our cycle. It's not wrong or bad or negative: it's just when our energy wanes and calls us inwards.

The moon lives with the sacred and once-revered shadow, and so do we.

**When we acknowledge our shadow,
it's wise, self-healing and healthy.**

Suppressed shadow, however, distorts and manifests as imbalance. And the imbalanced shadow is what leads to both emotional and physical pain and dis-ease.

Most of us avoid our shadows, because that's where shame, 'issues' and symptoms live.

We think these symptoms are 'bad'; but really, they're just our body's way of getting our attention and sending us signs and messages. In this way, our symptoms become highly revealing insights into what our bodies and psyches need in order to be in balance.

Know that as a woman, your shadow holds all the keys to what keeps you small and holds you back. And your shadow doesn't discriminate. She affects every facet of your being; and she'll keep prodding and poking until you realize that all the things you try so hard to avoid are *actually* the very things that will set you free.

So how do we begin to heal this? How do we connect with source?

First, we have to make sure our wombs are able to receive. Sometimes we can have a build-up of energy, or absorb projections of what it is to be a woman – to be a witch. We absorb these projections consciously and unconsciously from the media, from men, from other women, from culture and from society, then hold them as emotions in our womb space.

The way we feel about this space – about our periods, bleeding and not bleeding, our wants and desires – is ALL stored in our wombs. So much can, and does, get stored here, and it muffles SHE. It silences our connection to Shakti.

∽ How to Cleanse ∾ Your Womb Space

Do this anytime, apart from when you're bleeding.

what to do
Take a few breaths. Place one hand on your heart, and the other on your womb space.

Allow your awareness to settle into your womb area.

Follow your breath, in and out.

Follow the third breath down inside your body, and let it rest in your womb.

What you're doing with this is oxygenating this entire area. When you do that, you move the *prana* and energy in your womb space, so that anything that was stuck or stagnating can be dislodged and removed.

On the next in-breath, tighten your pelvic floor muscles and extend that connection into your womb area. Go gently, though: you're not doing a vag workout.

Then on your out-breath, relax. This moves the energy in your womb space, and dislodges any energy that doesn't belong in there.

As you're doing this, set your intention, e.g. 'I now release the energy of my ex-lover/trauma/an experience.'

Start to notice what's happening. You're not looking for anything specific, and you don't need to reach out and fix anything either. Just keep a gentle rhythm going: in-breath tighten, out-breath release.

As 'stuff' is dislodged, you may start to feel residue from the relationships/experience, entanglements or emotions.

Sometimes we can feel the emotions, witness them, and then get stuck thinking they're real and that we can't work with them. Really though? They're simply a memory making itself available. So just witness it and let it go.

Sometimes the emotion won't come up right away either. Instead, it'll get a bit dislodged. Then when you next bleed, you'll clear the residue of this particular dislodging.

Do this for 5–10 minutes. Journal whatever comes up for you.

∽⌒⊙⌒∾

Body Talk

What's your relationship with your body?

How do you FEEL residing in her?

This is such a loaded question for women; and it's a big reason so many of us are scared to really go there – to meet with the fear and resistance of letting our truth be fully expressed. It's because we don't trust ourselves; and most importantly, we don't trust our bodies.

This is a whole other book/conversation/unfolding, but we NEED to meet with that resistance in order to understand how we got to this place.

Before we do though, there's something you NEED to know.

It's NOT your fault.
I repeat, it's NOT YOUR FAULT.

You've been conditioned to seek the answers to EVERYTHING outside of yourself, when everything you'll ever need is inside.

You've been so disconnected from your body that you no longer have a barometer to FEEL what's real and true.

And the thing is, a woman's body is THE only barometer she'll EVER need in order to FEEL what's real and true.

So before you allow your inner bitch to RAGE at the way in which we've ALL been 'played', I want you to meet yourself where you are.

I want you to meet yourself right where you are and unfurl.

I don't want you to wait 'til you've 'got the answers' or you have it all 'figured out'. (And your inner perfectionist will *hate* me for that.)

Instead, I want you to find a really sticky, uncomfortable place; and I want you to explore it, right now. And even though I'm SURE you'll want to skip this or find something else to do, I urge you to set aside half an hour and show up for yourself.

It's something I do often.

In the dark part of the year, usually just before Imbolc, I run an online RE:WILDING programme. I invite women to show up and immerse themselves in the dark – both of the season and of the not knowing – and we explore all of this because this is the 'material'. This is the stuff that we work with.

I urge you to meet yourself wherever you're at now in relationship to your body, and practise it too.

Here's what I wrote in the RE:WILDING circle earlier this year in response to the question: *Right now, what's your body story?*

'My nervous system is in overdrive – I've had migraines, been sick daily, moved into my head and out of my body where doubt and fear and not-good-enough reign.

I keep apologizing.

For EVERYTHING.

I felt like a total fucking fraud. I'm talking about wild and feminine nature, yet I'm not feeling wild and free AT ALL. I'm feeling constricted and restricted and running away sounds far more appealing than running with the fucking wolves.

Then I realized that I wasn't creating RE:WILDING. I was experiencing RE:WILDING and it was consuming me.

It was showing me its full spectrum. All the things we're experiencing on a daily basis as a woman – restriction, fear, doubt, not-good-enough, too much. ALL OF IT.

It was showing what it is to show up unfinished. Undone.

I didn't show up fully yesterday. I put on a face because I thought I had to have my shit together. Over 200 women have signed up: all of them looking to me to guide them in this work, and I couldn't get out of bed because my adrenals were fucked and I'm hating on myself for feeling so small, for not trusting myself or listening to my body wisdom despite teaching that very thing.

This is ALL REWILDING.

Being the FULL expression of woman.

When the moon went full last night, I felt a shift in my entire body.

I slept alone. I often do on the dark and full moon. My energy gets MASSSIVE and all-consuming; and this morning, I woke up, the sun was shining, I went for a walk in nature and I feel love in my body again.

This is the way of REWILDING.

It's scary to show up whole.

And by whole, I mean messy, scared, uncontrollable, happy and contradictory. But this is why we have this time together, to explore it all. To feel it all.

To express.

To vent.

To dance with it all.

And to know that it's not a fix-it process: it's an exploration, and we're in it together.

So I ask you the same question: *Right now, what's your body story?*

And I don't want you to overthink or edit yourself. I just want you to take three deep-down-into-your-womb breaths, and then allow yourself to write/draw/express the first thing that makes itself known to you.

Don't try and fix it, or reason with it. Just meet it, heart and womb on.

Fiercely and with compassion for yourself in the process.

Allow yourself to come undone and use creative expression as a way in which you let that un-done-ness have a voice.

Please, if you're called, share what you've written and/or what comes up for you in circle – ask for help or ask to be witnessed.

Whatever the story, I need you to know that you are loved.

SO. MUCH.

The Eve Stain

The Eve Stain happens to everyone – men and women – but particularly women. It's the stain of sin, which is essentially shame. It comes in the way we're looked at and talked about. It's what's assumed about us as women.

And it sticks.

It sticks in our psyches because we're not initiated into our power at menarche. It sticks because our bleeding years aren't celebrated as the unfolding of our cyclic powers and feminine wisdom. It sticks because childbirth isn't seen as the incredible spiritual and creative act that it absolutely is.

And it sticks because, when we stop bleeding, we're told that we're surplus to requirements; when actually, we're women who no longer need to unfold and unfurl. We are sovereigns. We are queens. We are wild. We are crones and we are wise women.

This stain of shame has meant that we've unknowingly abandoned our centre, our Shakti and our connection to source. This loss, this disconnection, is at the root of *all* our feelings of fear, not-good-enough and unworthiness.

Yet the Shakti at the heart of us embraces all of this and more. It's the part of us that pursues our deepest pleasure and thrives on it. It's the part that we often shrink from.

Now, the dictionary won't tell you the *real* definition of sensuality, desire and pleasure.

It won't tell you that your one-way ticket to bliss involves entering life through your senses, and attuning yourself to what *is*. Why? Because pleasure is yet another thing Patriarchy has systematically separated us from. That's how the distorted, masculine energy took over the planet: by subduing, turning off, turning down and making us distrust and feel ashamed of our own desires.

Pleasure has been relegated to sexuality; and when and if we *do* talk about it, we only talk about orgasming. Yet pleasure? Well that is multi-freakin' deliciously dimensional.

Forget the watered-down, palatable version of pleasure you've been sold. The Sorceress wants you to explore *real* pleasure: the wild, untameable version.

Claim YOUR pleasure.

Self-Sourcing

'All acts of love and pleasure are my rituals.'
— DOREEN VALIENTE

Pleasure shows itself to me in many forms: a hot bath, salted caramel raw chocolate, a delicious orgasm, having my nails painted, cuddles, belly dancing, fresh flowers, dry body brushing, silence, big redwood trees, swimming in the ocean, a massage, eating figs, SHE Flow yoga, listening to boy bands (yes, still), beautiful ritual, drinking tea, the smell of jasmine, a spa…

I could go on for days listing all the things that bring me pleasure. I take serious props from High Priestess Doreen: sourcing my pleasure in ALL its forms is definitely my most favourite kind of magic.

When I talk about the act of self-sourcing with clients and in workshops, the initial reaction is that it sounds self-indulgent and selfish. Women are so used to putting others before themselves that their own wants and needs come WAY down the list.

Once again, I get it: these are old patterns and conditioning I'm asking you to unpick and unravel. But to love yourself fiercely – to self-source in a world where women are taught that they don't matter enough to be top of their own list of priorities – is actually really bloody radical.

Self-sourcing will liberate you.

When you *know* what you want, desire and need, when you *know* what brings you deep pleasure, and when you *know* how to source it and call it in, without looking for anyone else's help? (Yep, even for body-shaking orgasms: creating those on your own is a paradigm-changer!) It breaks the chains of disempowerment. It breaks the demonizing of the female body. And it reconnects you to your true nature, to Source.

It calls you to take the centre stage of your own life.

✧ THE CHARMED AND DANGEROUS SPRITZER

This Charmed and Dangerous Spritzer was one of the first mists I ever sold as The SASSY Sorceress. Use *this* essence to remember *your* essence.

What you'll need:

- Distilled water or 100-proof vodka
- 9 drops ginger essential oil
- 9 drops orange essential oil
- 7 drops cinnamon essential oil
- 11 drops lavender essential oil
- 13 drops bergamot essential oil
- Glass spray bottle

What to do:

Under a waning or dark moon, add 80ml/3fl oz of vodka/distilled water to a 120ml/4fl oz bottle.

Add the oils with love and intention, while repeating the mantra, 'I am charmed and dangerous, I am Sorceress.'

Place the lid on the bottle, and shake well to combine the contents.

Lightly mist your body, your bedroom, your sacred space or your yoga mat.

✧

Loving on me is the greatest magic I can create. It doesn't matter whether I'm:

… buying myself a crystal rose quartz yoni wand to bring myself to orgasm

… making an essence that anchors me into my truth

… taking time to create whole, nourishing food instead of ordering a take away

… finding a massage therapist who understands the complexity of my tilted pelvis and hyper-flexibility

… rescheduling an appointment because I'm on Day 28 of my menstrual cycle

… or organizing my finances so I know what I'm earning and what I'm spending

Regardless of HOW I'm loving on myself, it's radical – because with every act of self-sourcing, I recognize that I matter and that I'm worthy enough to call in what I need, want and desire. In the bedroom, in relationships, in work and in life.

You are worthy of calling in what you need, want and desire. Just so you know.

⤳ Source Yourself ⤲

Make a list of all the things that you want, need and desire.

Look at all the ways that you could make it possible to receive, allow or make them available in your life.

Pick one item a week (actually, you can pick as many as you want; but if you're new to receiving and accepting, one is plenty to begin with), and actively make it happen without guilt or apology.

You're a creatrix, and it's your birthright to self-source.

You've got this.

⤳⤲

Celebrating, Honouring and Initiating You

When you acknowledge, trust and find ways to feel good about being in your body, you no longer try to escape it or resist its teachings. You know with certainty that, despite what you've been told, your pleasure, desire and sensuality are NOT evil. You know that what lies between your thighs is actually your direct connection to Source.

Your power.

As witches, we self-source, create ritual and celebrate our bodies so that when other women – and men – spend time in our presence and our wholeness, they remember themselves too.

I'm in this one with you. I haven't got it figured out. Not one little bit.

But what I know for sure is that I'm doing the work. I'm meeting new edges. EVERY. FREAKIN'. DAY.

I'm finding myself in the dark and the not knowing, and learning to get really comfortable with it. I'm meeting parts of me I don't like and not rushing to fix them. Instead, I'm being totally open and willing to shed what no longer serves me.

The old stories that have been buried deep in our psyches – all the mistruths about our bodies and who we are as women – must be witnessed, fully felt and then let go of if we are fully to reclaim our connection to our bodies, our pleasure and our desires.

Let's dare to be the Sorceress – SHE Who Is Charmed, Dangerous and Not Afraid of the Dark – without fear of repercussion. Let's silence the voices that say we're drawing far too much attention to ourselves, that we're taking up too much space, or that we'll be abandoned because we shine too fucking bright.

Let's live a life undone.

Don't hold back, push down or suppress ANYTHING. Feel – and express – it all.

You are a Sorceress.

I am a Sorceress.

The 'Wake the Witch' Project

Invoke SHE Who Is Charmed, Dangerous and Not Afraid of the Dark by:

Getting comfortable with the dark: literally. In some shamanic traditions, initiating a person into their power involves them spending a night in a forest or other sacred place alone.

Finding a way to be in the physical darkness, on your own, for a period of time is really powerful.

Rediscovering sensuality: or indulge it if you're already in touch with it. A partner (or more than one) is nice, but not necessary. Read Anaïs Nin, or any other book that makes you contemplate your sexual nature, or just expand beyond what you've been willing to try or reflect on before. You can find lots of practices in my book *Love Your Lady Landscape*.

Being resourceful: the 'Source'ress is resourceful and she encourages you to use all your tools. You have access to so many: spell creation, manifestation, alchemy – to get what you want, need and desire.

Not because you're selfish or manipulative, but because you're putting yourself first. If you cringe or wince at this idea, keep saying it and doing it until you don't. When you're fully in service to yourself – when you're nourished and pleasured and your needs are met – you are, by your very nature, in service to SHE.

And that, witch, is real magic.

Chapter 13

The Witch Has Woken

I am woken, not broken.

*'We're connected, as women. It's like a
spiderweb. If one part of that web vibrates, if
there's trouble, we all know it, but most of the
time we're just too scared, or insecure to help.
But if we don't help each other, who will?'*

— SARAH ADDISON ALLEN, THE PEACH KEEPER

Witches, what I've shared in this book is to wake you, not break you.

It's to wake you in the womb.

It's to wake your wild and feminine nature.

It's to wake your power, your inner authority and your Goddess-given sovereignty.

Because honestly, there's nothing more important than that right now. Nothing.

To be awake to what's REALLY going on here – a world in crisis, a world that's being destroyed by an unhealthy, masculine ego, a world where women have been stripped of their power, their rights and their agency – is to be a witch, burning.

A witch burning with rage and anger.

A witch burning with passion and determination.

A witch burning with compassion and love.

Witch, we walk in fire, because we ARE the fire.

The thing they used to destroy us during the 'witch craze' is the very thing that will wake us now. We are Shakti, we are the destroyer, we are the nurturer, we are kundalini rising, and we are the light in the dark.

Become a living fire of transformation.

Feel.

The.

Burn.

Great Mumma, SHE, consider this burning an invocation.

Show us ALL the ways in which to remember, honour and revere you in our current female, human form.

Now, THIS is the magic your cauldron was made for.

Get angry and rage-full at the injustice of all that has gone before. Feel it in every cell. Be willing to do the work that needs to be done to heal it.

ALL OF IT.

That work? It starts and ends with you, BTW.

Remember all the parts of your wild and feminine nature that have been placed in the dark.

Reconnect with Mumma Nature, your body and truth.

Reclaim what's rightfully yours, starting with your menstrual cycle, and declare that shit sacred.

Revere it all. The mess, the truth, the polarities, the paradoxes, the Mystery and EVERYTHING in between.

Do it all with fierce love and compassion, the like of which has never been seen – or most importantly felt – before.

When each and every woman feels the burn in this way – when she stirs this remembrance, reconnection, reclamation and reverence in the heat and flames of her cauldron – alchemy occurs.

She heals.

She heals her personal wounds and those of the collective.

She takes responsibility for her nourishment, pleasure, boundaries and desires.

She becomes self-sourced and can re-source the Earth, because she knows that what she stands on is what she stands for.

She wakes. Fully.

And together we all create an epic pussy-storm of SHE-infused Mumma love. The fierce, powerful and much-needed compassionate kind of love that we (men and women) are ALL craving.

Yoohooooo, Patriarchy! Guess what? Mumma's home.

NOTE: we evoke this power so that we can recognize that the men in our lives are NOT the Patriarchy. We acknowledge that it's unproductive and not at all helpful to keep blaming them – consciously or subconsciously. And we acknowledge that when we know what it feels like to reclaim and fully own our power, we will then help them to meet us where *we* are at with clear communication, guidance, patience and love.

Sisterhood

> *'I won't fight other women for one of the
> limited seats at the table. We'll march side
> by side and demand a bigger table.'*
> – GLENNON DOYLE MELTON

Witch, you're not in this alone.

While your stories and your experiences are unique to you, we're all connected. And not one of us can burn this shit down – old stories, patriarchal conditioning, self-sabotaging beliefs – alone. We need each other to do this work. This witch work.

I sometimes forget that I don't have to, nor can I, do this work solo.

Yes, I sat down and wrote words on a page to make this book; but it's what we do together – calling our power back, creating evolution and starting revolutions in and from our womb space – that creates the real magic.

Asking for help from another woman, sitting in circle with other women, trusting another woman with your story, exposing your vulnerability in front of another woman? These are all acts of serious defiance and rebellion.

Why?

Because we've been told over and over, in a million different ways, that we're unworthy, that we're undeserving and that we have no value.

It's in our DNA and programming to find other women untrustworthy. Many of us have personal experiences of another woman competing/ stealing from us/stabbing us in the back.

We have to tear this shit down.

We have to help each other first to trust ourselves, our intuition and our inner authority. To create a world where we not only feel love and pride for our bodies and who we are in them, but also a world where we feel safe fully inhabiting those bodies without fear or worry of harm coming to them when we walk down the street.

Then, slowly, and with deep, deep compassion (because, again, we *will* fuck this up, over and over again), we have to find ways to start trusting each other again.

That's why I create online and in-person covens, retreats and temple spaces – so that women can circle with other amazing women to unearth, explore and unravel this experience. To dismantle our armour, and to find our way back to trust. Trust in ourselves and in each other.

We witness and we're witnessed, we support and we're supported, we learn and we teach. There's often body-wracking wails and belly-shaking laughter too.

And together we grow strong roots, so that together we can burn away the old stories, beliefs and untruths; and rise up strong, supported and in our power. Our SHE power. Whole.

Gather the Women

Don't wait for someone else to do it. Gather the women yourself.

I began by gathering women together for SHE ceremonies in my front room.

We met on the dark moon, set up a sacred space, and all placed items on the altar to be charged.

We let go of outside perceptions through breath work, and smudged and cleansed ourselves and the space. We called in the elements and opened the circle. We moved our bodies in a SHE Flow Yoga practice (non-linear movement that nourishes the feminine body), drank ceremonial cacao sacrament and allowed what needed to be felt to be felt. We created art, entered into radical rest with yoga nidra, and then shared stories, listened deeply and witnessed each other.

When our time together came to an end, we thanked each other with the biggest love and gratitude, closed the circle and shared food together to ground ourselves back in this world.

Some call this a red tent, some call it a coven and some call it a moon temple. I call it women gathering – and we need to do more of it, because when women gather, magic happens and revolutions start. They've separated us, disconnected us from ourselves and each other because they know that it's when we gather together and share, that we are truly powerful.

Call back your power, call back our power. Do the same, do it differently, but DO gather.

Women, please gather.

Witch, Do It Your Way

I'm a blood witch, I'm a self-initiated witch, I'm a witch of the ancient ways and I'm a witch who lives in the 21st century. I'm a feminist, an activist and a mother who hasn't birthed a child.

I am a witch who has woken. I'm a woman who's looking at the world around her and finally saying, 'I know why this is broken.'

261

My wish and intention is that within the pages of this book you find a phrase, a practice, a suggestion, a quote or a story that ignites the fire in you. One that wakes you up. One that calls you to reclaim your power. One that makes you want to take back what's rightfully yours.

The rest?

Well, that's down to *you*.

Don't let anyone tell you HOW to be a witch.

You can be a witch who casts spells. Or not.

You can be a witch who uses herbs and essential oils. Or not.

You can be a witch who has an altar. Or not.

You can be a witch who is political. Or not.

You can be a witch who makes art. Or not.

Question the gurus and the teachers. Question this book. Question everything.

Seek the truth in ALL things. Starting with you.

Make your own rules. Then break them.

Be the woman you are here to be in this lifetime.

Witch: Unleashed. Untamed. Unapologetic.

Wake up! You are it.

You are a part of the
circle of the Wise.

There is no mystery that has not
already been revealed to you.

There is no power you do
not already have.

– Starhawk

⤳ Closing Circle ⤴

Close your eyes. Take a deep breath. Relax your hands, palms face up. We're closing the circle of our magical workings and returning to our everyday lives.

Ancestors, witches and wise women who've gone before us, thank you for joining us, sitting with us and guiding us in circle.

SHE, divine feminine, lady of all that is, thank you for your presence and your blessing. Thanks for clearing the space of any heavy energy; and filling it with love, healing and truth.

SHE, I thank you for working through me, working through us, and making sure we heard and felt what we needed the most as we experienced this circle together.

Blessed be.

As I call in each quarter, turn to face that direction. We'll be going widdershins (anti-clockwise) – starting in the West.

> **To the West, element of Water.** *Thank you for cleansing us, quenching our thirst, nourishing us, allowing us to explore the ebb and flow of our emotions, and purifying our thoughts.*
>
> *Hail and farewell.*
>
> **To the South, element of Fire.** *Thank you for burning away regrets, igniting a fire of passion and desire and for being the flame that ignites the light of others when plunged into darkness.*
>
> *Hail and farewell.*
>
> **To the East, element of Air.** *Thank you for blowing out the old and bringing in the new. Thank you for helping us to allow the winds of change and not resist them.*
>
> *Hail and farewell.*
>
> **To the North, element of Earth.** *Thank you for holding us and supporting us as we grow strong roots so that we can rise.*
>
> *Hail and farewell.*
>
> **Mumma Earth, Father Sky, Grandmumma Moon, Grandfather Sun, Star Nations and the Mysteries that lie in between.** *Thank you for being present, supporting us and guiding us in our circle.*

⤳⤴

By the Air that is Her Breath
By the Fire of Her bright Spirit
By the Waters of Her Womb
By the Earth that is her Body

May the circle be open but never unbroken
May the love of the Goddess
Be ever in your heart.

Merry meet,
And merry part,
And merry meet again.

Blessed Be.

The 'Wake the Witch' Bookshelf

Because if you're anything like me, you'll have been highlighting and making notes of the parts in the book you now want to go and find out more about, am I right?

Here are the books I've referred to and think you'll love:

- Achterberg, Jeanne – *Woman as Healer*
- Bennett, Jessica – *Feminist Fight Club*
- Beth, Rae – *Hedge Witch: A Guide to Solitary Witchcraft*
- Bird, Stephanie Rose – *Sticks, Stones, Roots and Bones*
- Boland, Yasmin – *Moonology*
- Federici, Silvia – *Caliban and the Witch*
- Leek, Sybil – *Diary of a Witch*
- Leek, Sybil – *The Complete Art of Witchcraft*
- Patterson, Rachel – *Grimoire of a Kitchen Witch*
- Perrone, Bobette – *Medicine Women, Curanderas and Women Doctors*
- Romm, Aviva – *Botanical Medicine for Women's Health*
- Shen, Ann – *Bad Girls Throughout History*

- Valiente, Doreen – *Natural Magic*
- Valiente, Doreen – *Witchcraft for Tomorrow*
- Wood, Gail – *Shamanic Witch: Spiritual Practice Rooted in the Earth and Other Realms*
- Worwood, Valerie Ann – *The Fragrant Pharmacy*

Tools

My big wish for this book is that, within its pages, you'll find what you need to begin to wake the witch, reclaim your power and become your own magic-making oracle.

Here are other ways to help you go deeper and find other witches on the same path.

www.wakethewitches.com

Go to www.wakethewitches.com for more information on the tools, rituals and ceremonies mentioned throughout the book.

There's a Wake the Witches playlist and soundscape to listen to. There's also a Wake the Witches podcast series for you to tune in to and get inspired by; and a free Wake the Witches zine to download and print out. It's filled with cauldron conversations, insights and magic from some of my favourite witches. Basically, I've got *all* your witchy needs covered.

#wakethewitches

Please share while you read the book – I love knowing where you're reading it, and what's coming up for you as you read. Use the hashtag #wakethewitches on social media.

(I spend most of my time on Instagram, so come follow me! I'm @sassylisalister)

Wake The Witches Workshops

Experience opportunities – either in-person or online – to wake and reclaim the witch.

These workshops are where practical magic meets deep feminine wisdom. They're what our witchy hearts and wombs are hungry for: the good stuff.

To find out more, go to: www.wakethewitches.com/events

Join the SHE Coven

Join the SHE coven – an online community – to experience monthly moon rituals and spells, intuitive insight and tools to tap into your personal power. You'll also have access to a private coven filled with waking witches reclaiming their power across the globe.

To join, go to: www.wakethewitches.com/SHEcoven

Acknowledgements

Big love, broomsticks and magic spells of gratitude are being sent to these very wise, wonderful and wild witches:

The Viking, Rich Lister – living with this witch isn't easy; and it takes an awakened, soul-filled, strong and big-hearted man to hold space, support, nurture, appreciate and love on the wildness and unravelling that is THIS particular womb witch. Thank you for being the truest example of love and masculinity. Oh, and thanks for being hot and having a beard. That helps too.

The witches/ancestors/women who've gone before me – Nanna Riley, Nanna Clark, the Mumma and all those I've never met in the flesh but have spent time with in visions, in circle and in dreamtime.

I feel you at my back.

Deep, deep bows of gratitude.

My Maltese Dreamers – Lisa Caddock, Amy Humphries, Heather Blanchard, Meghan Field, Clare Fairhurst, Ebonie Allard and Zoe Charles – for hearing The Call, coming to Ma Malta with me and creating some fierce full moon magic in temple together which birthed this book.

Fam Lister – I know it's not easy welcoming a witch into the fam, but I'm beyond grateful that you let me hold rituals in your forest, keep the broomstick on standby and grow ALL the herbs. Seriously, I'm so blessed to call you my family.

David Wells – for being THE best cheerleader and EVER. Astro guidance, random texts, ridiculously healthy lunches (yawn) with a side helping of bitch are what got this book finished. That's an actual fact. Love you, mister.

Susie Rains and Aimee Richards Welton – for having the patience of ALL the saints and angels, and loving me and supporting me despite the fact I've barely seen your beautiful faces for the last year as I've either been writing, editing or promoting a book. Thank you ×10000000000000. We can drink cocktails now. A LOT of cocktails.

Jenny Gibbons, Root and Flower – for being the wisest witch, for knowing me deeply, for our long conversations and for making beautiful prods that made my writing process feel so much more delicious. I love you and all that you do, lady.

Carrie Anne Moss – for joining me while this book was being written in Glastonbury for a magical adventure, for your wise, deep and powerful truth telling and for your big, generous heart. ALL THE LOVE.

Ani Richardson – for always supporting, loving and inspiring me. ALWAYS. I love you, ladylove.

Sarah Durham Wilson – for being my coven sister this lifetime, and many lifetimes before. Thank the goddess for you in my life.

Maya Hackett – for your relentless medicine and wisdom sharing, for your hand (and heart) holding, and for sharing what you share in the world (and selfishly, for what you share with me).

Red Lady, Meggan Watterson – for always knowing what to say. Always. Your words have always been, and always will be, a balm for my red soul.

Katie Brockhurst – for bloody everything. The love, the advice, the support, the FaceTime dates, the tears and the laughter. Thanks for being my best witch – here's to a lifetime of adventures together!

Lucy Sheridan – for being a hand-holder, love-giver and back-rubber in the conception of this book. Thanks for making/encouraging/ supporting me to do it. Also thanks for introducing me to garlic butter on my Padana – life has seriously never been the same since. Love you, woman.

Team Hay House – for daring to publish words that weren't always easy to share, and for supporting the witch waking up. You're ALL amazing.

Word witch editors, Tamara and Tanja – women, you have skills. Undeniable skills. Thanks for making what can often be a painful task, actually really bloody enjoyable. Thanks for your insight, knowledge and word wisdom, but mainly thanks for Tuesday night/Wednesday morning edit parties. We made the 84-hour time difference totally work. Ahem. Seriously, we are proof that real magic can happen when three witches gather together. Love you both VERY much.

Hollie Holden – thanks for reminding me that I was only ever writing this book for you. Phew. Amy Kiberd and Rebecca Campbell – for all the calls, texts, rituals, tears, talks and laughter, I love you. Holly, thanks for reminding me that I was never actually writing this book for any one other than you. Phew.

Dana Gillespie and Holly Grigg-Spall – together we are the Holy freakin' womb Trinity – thanks for the incredible support and love that you two LA ladies give to me in ALL the ways.

YOU – to all the women who sent emails and messages saying they'd pre-ordered this book before it had even been written, to all the women who reminded me why I was writing the book when I felt my voice being silenced, over and over. And to all the witches who are waking and ready to do the work, who I share space with every day in the techno coven that is social media – thank you. Thank you with all my witchy heart for showing up. For me, for you, for SHE and for the entire freakin' world.

We need your magic. Really.